I0560773

THE STORMS OF OUR LIVES

RUSSELL HARPER II

"If God is for us, who can be against us?"
Romans 8:31

All inquiries should be addressed to:

Book Domain LLC.
543 E Louise Dr Phoenix, Az 85050

Ordering Information:
Amount Deals. Special rebates are accessible on the amount bought by corporations, associations, and others. For points of interest, contact the distributor at the address above.

Printed in the United States of America.

ISBN-13   Paperback   978-1-967903-85-6
            eBook   978-1-967903-84-9

Library of Congress Control Number: xxxx

CONTENTS

PART 2

GOD'S PROTECTION

PART 3

GOD'S PLAN

PART 4

SALVATION AND YOUR WALK

4 My message and my preaching were not with wise and persuasive words, but with a demonstration of the Spirit's power, **5** so that your faith might not rest on human wisdom, but on God's power.

1 Cor. 2:4–5 NIV

1. Therefore, since through God's mercy we have this ministry, we do not lose heart. 2. Rather, we have renounced secret and shameful ways; we do not use deception, nor do we distort the word of God. On the contrary, by setting forth the truth plainly we commend ourselves to everyone's conscience in the sight of God.

2 Cor. 4:1–2 NIV

MY LIFE—THE LIGHT AT THE END OF THE TUNNEL

When I was growing up my old man used to say I could see the "Light at the end of the tunnel." You might just think of it as a joke, or just a sly remark but I always listen to words, and the favorite phrase I had when my dad would say things like that is "what do you mean by that dad?" or "what does that mean?"

Well, the older I got, the more I used those words for what they really meant. I speak English and like every language, it is a beautiful art to know, especially when they are interesting or kind words spoken or written. So, when "I" say were almost at the end of the tunnel or were getting close to the end of the tunnel it usually means I'm just about finished or we are literally going through a tunnel and we are about to come out the other end!

Lately I have been seeing that light at the end of the tunnel in a whole "new" light. It's sort of is, when I was at Church camp so, so, many years ago. I think I was 13 years old maybe younger but I listened to the minister over and over again we sat on a hill they called Vespers and the minister would come out to that stick cross in the middle of a laid down concrete cross, and all of us kids would come out year after year. This went on for a few years and like kids are, we were bored stiff, if that's what you called it in those days.

We really didn't pay attention; at least I didn't think we were. I would set there with my legs crossed, and play with the sticks that were laying in that yard digging holes with them.

All of the sudden a light came on in the middle of that tunnel just like the one Dad always talked about. All those sermons that I didn't think I heard, all the stories in the Bible came into that light and like a solid beam of light, it hit me. It wasn't enough to just sit there and listen, I felt the hunger for it, I felt it, I saw the light at the end of the tunnel and I broke through to the other end!

When I made that decision to give that "Free Will" back to the Lord and asked him into my heart, I couldn't stop, the stories that were alive in me and it wasn't enough to hear, feel or see, I knew I needed to act on them. You couldn't pull the Bible away from me. You couldn't taint the water at my baptism in the Lake; no I felt like I was there with John the Baptist. I knew the Holy Spirit was there! Just like these words can testify to the fact that the Lord speaks to me today. I wanted to live in that moment all of my days. I was Hungry for the word I hung on every spiritual thing ever said to me. I ask myself what you do with this. I wish that, that strength stayed with me and shown itself when I needed it most.

At this age today and even what I have been into and through I can say unequivocally he has never left me, he has "always" been there by my side, in my heart and in my mind and of course in my soul.

I fell and stumbled and looked death in the face, I have seen things and done things I can't take back but the Lord never left, I could feel his tears when I turned around, but I also felt his hand on my shoulder each and every time I struggled with anything that I faced.

I have a wife now that share those struggles and she shares my gift, we are a one in the same flesh. I share Gods gifts. When He speaks to me, I act. When he wants me to paint, I paint. When He wants me to write, whether on paper, computer or even text, I write. This is where I meet our Lord. YFICA Russ

Pass on this good news, use your gifts and be freer than you will ever imagine! I am on the other end of that tunnel and I don't ever want to go back in!

From Abraham to Moses, from Isaiah to the son of God, from a Virgin named Mary until Jesus death on the cross for all our sin. From the least of lies to the worst of sin ever thought of, "all sin" for everyone for all time. He freely gives us life after death to those who believe in him and confess their sins to him. John 3:16 says it all "For God so loved the world that he gave his one and only Son, that whoever believes in him shall not perish but have eternal life."

Do you think that the things we have done will keep us out of his grace?

9 For in Christ all the fullness of the Deity lives in bodily form, 10 and in Christ you have been brought to fullness. He is the head over every power and authority. 11 In him you were also circumcised with a circumcision not performed by human hands. Your whole self ruled by the flesh[b] was put off when you were circumcised by[c] Christ, 12 having been buried with him in baptism, in which you were also raised with him through your faith in the working of God, who raised him from the dead.

13 When you were dead in your sins and in the uncircumcision of your flesh, God made you[d] alive with Christ. He forgave us all our sins, 14 having canceled the charge of our legal indebtedness, which stood against us and condemned us; he has taken it away, nailing it to the cross.

THE EYE OF A STORM

I heard the song "Eye of the Storm" by Ryan Stevenson, the other day.

I started thinking about my Navy days. Back in 1975 I saw the eye of a storm in the middle of the night we were going through a typhoon! I was young, 19 as a matter of fact and thought, at that time, that this Destroyer, (my home for about four years), was indeed my sanctuary and was invincible. The USS England was 533 feet long, 54 feet wide built of iron, steel through and through, and weighed 7800 tons. I was one of the few that worked in the most dangerous place in the ship, the Fireroom! Picture a sealed coffee pot full of water and steam and now its rocking back and forth.

There were ten to fifteen of us for each of those two spaces. Our ship was rocking back and forth to the tune of about 25 to 38 degree rolls.

Well let's get back to the storm. Our mess decks were being tore up in preparation for a yard period so when I had to get from one fireroom to the other I had to go topside I held on pretty tight to those lifelines and that's when I saw the eye of the storm it was like we were out of it but then I looked up at the sky and it seemed like I was looking through a big tube with the moon in the middle. It was sort of still out and the temperature was tropic. I knew I had to get back to the other fireroom so I went on down. About that, time the rocking got vicious again and like I said, I was young back then and this was just another adventure to me. It turned out that I indeed had seen the eye of the storm, it was rough getting into, calm in the middle and rough getting out of that storm off the coast of Korea, all those years ago.

One thing you learn going into a storm is, it's a rough decision to go in, but sometimes you can't go around it. Then we are given an eye, a timeout in the middle of it, on our way through, it prepares you to go through to the other side. "One thing I forgot to mention about these storms, Typhoons, Tornadoes, or Hurricanes, these storms travel and if your moving in the same direction you will find yourself in that storm a lot longer, unless it dies out."

The storms of life work the same way; going into them are rough, painful and sometimes hurtful. If you get to the eye, you have the time to reflect on things that have happened, how you got there, how you get out, and time to heal before moving ahead. Then you have to exit, "push through to the other side," you learn from the situation and choose the right direction to leave it so you're not in there any longer than you have to and end up at right place so you don't end up on the rocks or run a ground, or just end up sunk.

Whatever you are going through, whatever pain, sin, loss or turmoil is crippling you, we have someone on the inside, through the rough times or through the eye of the storm and He helps you through the rough times coming out of any and all situations that is in your storm.

Before you start saying to yourself "this is my storm", "I own it," "it's my grief, "or "you don't know what I'm feeling," Think about this; the one who gave it all, yes I said ALL, and may I remind you of that story. About the Storm of all storms, the real "Perfect Storm," Gods only son Jesus went through that storm and planned his entrance and exit before any of us were ever born. It wasn't an easy escape, but one that will never be forgotten all in the name of Love.

So do you think your storm is so bad that you can't give it to the one that can take your burdens completely away, do you think you've done something so wrong that Jesus Christ sacrificed himself for a pick and choose?

1 John 1:5–10 says 5 This is the message we have heard from him and declare to you: God is light; in him there is no darkness at all. 6 If we claim to have fellowship with him and yet walk in the darkness,

we lie and do not live out the truth. 7 But if we walk in the light, as he is in the light, we have fellowship with one another, and the blood of Jesus, his Son, purifies us from all[a] sin.

8 If we claim to be without sin, we deceive ourselves and the truth is not in us. 9 If we confess our sins, he is faithful and just and will forgive us our sins and purify us from all unrighteousness. 10 If we claim we have not sinned, we make him out to be a liar and his word is not in us.

All of us need to know, Jesus loves us in our bad times and our good, no matter what the hurt, loss or sin is or was.

I have seen the eye of the storm and my storms, I gave it all to him that is the end of it, that's all the reminders and baggage that come to haunt us. We just give it all to him and let it go.

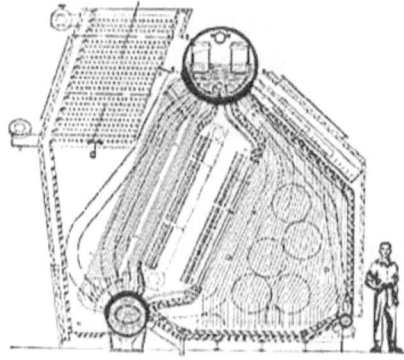

This is a 1200 PSI Boiler 1 of 4 onboard provide steam

PART 1

GOD'S POWERFUL WORD

A DOUBLE-EDGED SWORD

That is the real use of a sword, a double-edged sword? Well," back in those Days" that was usually the weapon of choice. It was probably brought about by the farmer's tools. Scythes that cut down stalks of grain and knives for cleaning fish. When there was an uprising and a fight broke out, they used those tools until they decided to turn them into weapons of war. Joel 3:10 Beat your plowshares into swords and your pruning hooks into spears. Let the weakling say, "I am strong!" So, a sword is the instrument of death and it was modified throughout the years to do its worst. They put two edges on the sword so it could cut and kill in multiple directions of the swing. They were Sharp just like the farmers tools had to be sharp, so were the instruments or tools of a soldier. I read this scripture of Romans today, (Paul's own words in his restless moments), and I really understood it more than ever. "Read it ever so slowly, it is not just a colorful way of describing a situation with the do's and do not's and more do's that are built into the New Testament." When you read it, it will touch your very soul. Things you asked forgiveness for, things that you haven't, your past, your plans for the day, those things that might slip into your mind, yes God has and will forgive you if you ask and believe, but when you read these word's, you may be convicted of things that might have slipped your mind but not the Holy Spirit's and the memory of your soul.

Romans 7:1, 5–24 (NIV) 15. I do not understand what I do. For what I want to do I do not do, but what I hate I do. 16. And if I do what I do not want to do, I agree that the law is good. 17. As it is, it is no longer I myself who do it, but it is sin living in me. 18. For I know that good itself does not dwell in me, that is, in my sinful nature. [a] For I have the desire to do what is good, but I cannot carry it out. 19. For I do not do the good I want to do, but the evil I do not want to do-this I keep on doing. 20. Now if I do what I do not want to do, it is no longer I who do it, but it is sin living in me that does it. 21. So I find this law at work: Although I want to do good, evil is right there with me. 22. For in my inner being I delight in God's law; 23. But I see another law at work in me, waging war against the law of my mind and making me a prisoner of the law of sin at work within me. 24. What a wretched man I am I Who will rescue me from this body that is subject to death?

So when you read Hebrews 4:12–16 (NIV), like everything else; read it and understand it, don't let worldly thought's creep into your mind. He is not speaking of a metal object that the world uses to literally cut through flesh, a spiritual sword that separates those worldly things such as the sin that Paul speaks of, it is the "world VS Gods righteousness." 4:12. For the word of God is a live and active. Sharper than any double-edged sword, it penetrates even to dividing soul and spirit, joints and marrow; it judges the thoughts and attitudes of the heart. 13. Nothing in all creation is hidden from God's sight. Everything is uncovered and laid bare before the eyes of him to whom we must give account.

I have felt that and l, being a believer have survived only because my Lord has given his son as a promise to me, to us and that price was heavier than any of us would or could imagine on a Cross.

When we read our Bibles as youth's we see the stories and the brave people of the ages. Life has not given us its experiences. We know right from wrong maybe depending on how we were brought up or how old we are. You know when the minister gives the sermon, the one where he says, "there is something in this book the Bible, for everyone," he might have said, that there is, "the good and the bad," but when I was young, I didn't get that part, the only thing I could grasp was the Good and those cool stories. When we read the Bible now that we have matured, we reach a point where that double edged sword is more than a definition of what the Old Testament had to offer as punishment back in those days. We have learned what Love really means, and we can all learn to love Jesus Christ the way he loves all of us unconditionally so much so that He died on a cross to free us from all our sin's. God didn't want it to come to this but he wanted us to come to him of our own free will and we can only be with God without sin.

All God ever wanted from us was Love and worship. So, as we see the pain now, we shake our heads and bow in shame. The good news is that, Jesus Christ arose from the grave! So, we lift our heads in Praise, while waiting for his return when he comes to take us home. We Are Not of This World, because we are Followers of the Highest' "Jesus Christ"

A STEADY CONSTANT

Happening all the time or very often over a period of time, staying the same, not changing, always loyal. Math is a constant but things change a little over time. Basic math doesn't change at all, you still have add, subtract, multiply, and divide _+-x.

You have a constant in your car, a steering wheel, gas or diesel, Power brakes, four or three wheels one or two do not steer the others do, headlights to see by night along with brake and running lights and turning signals that a lot of people still do not know exist. Most things have a constant or basic background at least it started some-where; but all "things" change! People change too, they change their minds, their clothes, cars, appearance, changes for the good and a lot for the bad. Have you ever noticed if you do a lot of good things, like helping people out of a tough time or going that extra mile for someone who needs gas or groceries, but then you get stopped, or picked up for speeding, jay walking or anything just once, you even admit it when your wrong, and then that one thing seems to stands out like a sore thumb. All of the sudden people get amnesia about those other things!

There is one common denominator that never changes! "One Steady Constant" that never gives in, always has your back, and never forgets the things you have done. You see those good things He never forgets There is a verse where God said in the end he will remember us all. Mathew 25:31–46 NIV "The Sheep and the Goats" 31. "When the Son of Man comes in his glory, and all the angels with him, he will sit on his glorious throne. 32. All the nations will be gathered before him, and he will separate the people one from another as a shepherd separates the sheep from the goats. 33. He will put the sheep on his right and the goats on his left. 34. "Then the King will say to those on his right, 'Come, you who are blessed by my Father; take your inheritance, the kingdom prepared for you since the creation of the world. 35. For I was hungry and you gave me something to eat, I was thirsty and you gave me something to drink, I was a stranger and you invited me in, 36. Needed clothes and you clothed me, I was sick and you looked after me, I was in prison and you came to visit me.' 37. "Then the righteous will answer him, 'Lord, when did we see you hungry and feed you, or thirsty and give you something to drink? 38. When did we see you a stranger and invite you in, or needing clothes and cloth you? 39. When did we see you sick or in prison and go to visit you?' 40. "The King will reply, 'Truly I tell you, whatever you did for one of the least of these brothers and sisters of mine, you did it for me.' 41. "Then he will say to those on his left, 'Depart from me, you who are cursed, into the eternal fire prepared for the devil and his angels. 42. For I was hungry and you gave me nothing to eat, I was thirsty and you gave me nothing to drink, 43. I was a stranger and you did not invite me in, I needed clothes and you did not clothe me, I was sick and in prison and you did not look after me.' 44. "They also will answer, 'Lord, when did we see you hungry or thirsty or a stranger or needing clothes or sick or in prison, and did not help you?' 45." He will reply, 'Truly I tell you, whatever you did not do for one of the least of these, you did not do for me.' 46. "Then they will go away to eternal punishment, but the righteous to eternal life."

You just don't want to get caught being a goat. You see he loves us unconditionally, that never changes. Since the beginning of time he has given us chances over and over again and again that never changes either. God, Jesus, the Holy Spirit has always been that one "steady constant". We are the ones that cannot stand still, the ones that have to have the next big thing, never satisfied with what we have already. Why not try listening to and for him to speak, find that quiet place, that still small voice that Elijah was listening for in the mountains. Be satisfied that we have a God, the only God that cares for us, his children.

BY THE BOOK

Have you ever noticed that a good lawyer has to know the English language better than most? They have to learn every word more literal than we do. They must know every meaning of every word brought up in court.

Sometimes I think Children at a certain age would make great lawyers. If you tell them not to do something and you don't word it perfectly and cover all your bases they will figure out some way for it to mean one thing and not the other. So I think we need to know that double standard and pray for the words of preparation, and then be prepared to use the Bible when the time comes with the help of the Holy Spirit and the full armor of God, we will be equipped to lead those that are lost out of the fog and into His loving arm and forgiveness that he paid such a price for.

—Coming to terms—

I think the hardest thing for nonbelievers or atheists to come to terms with, isn't that they do not believe there is "A GOD', I believe it is the fact that the acceptance of Christ in our lives is a simple act and that they're earthly thoughts are answering to the conviction of they're sin.

As I am sure we know, as followers of Jesus Christ, "at least I hope we have all come to terms with," is the fact that our God is in an "All

Knowing and an All-seeing God, and Becoming a Christian in all sense of the words is really quite simple.

To do so: Number one, we must Truly Believe in Jesus the Christ, that he is the flesh of God and walked the earth and was absolutely "sinless" The plan was and still is, to make a path for anyone to be with him in Heaven after our physical death He chose to allow himself to be the ultimate sacrifice by dying on a cross and taking all of our sins upon himself and then coming back after death which is exactly what he did, then you must believe this with all your Heart, soul and mind.

Number Two, the act of admitting your sin to Him and shedding the guilt by giving it all to God.

Number Three, start living a life for Him by simply spreading the word, this word, the story of how God planned this whole thing from the start of creation. As a believer you will have the help of a Holy Spirit that will give you guidance in all these teachings and when speaking to others. This in explanation is simple, but we have to always be on the lookout, because our enemy is fighting our hearts and minds into believing that this physical life is so much more important, please understand this: It is like a meal that is left to sit on a counter for a long time, soon everything will spoil; our physical bodies are only here for a short time, but with Christ we will have an eternity with him at the blink of an eye but only if we believe in him.

Whatever we have done on this earth, God has seen it all, "everything." He is asking like a mother or father with a child; just tell me what you did? He already knows it we just need to come to terms with it and admit to God that he already knows. He is saying "admit your sins that I have seen and Sin no more. Life will not always be easy but you will not be lugging around grudges, hatred or burdens because he is all you have to answer to and you will have an eternity with him. You will close your eyes one day and when they open, you will be looking into the eyes of Jesus the only one who loves you unconditionally—YFICA

HUMANITY VS GOD

I have the gift... of, "Gab," apparently on paper as well as speech. But as I grow older, the Lord has also given me wisdom and I firmly believe it is because he answers my prayer for wisdom. I will talk to just about anyone in my path about anything and especially about following our Savior Jesus Christ. The good Lord has gifted me not to always start a conversation but like the detective on a search through a phone call I listen more than speak and if I am patient the Lord will give me the right words or actions to keep that person on the line so the Lord can keep us on the same track, "so to speak". While I am sharing God, he is giving both me and the one I am speaking to, interaction through intercession. During these times I feel movement, real movement within my soul when a nonbeliever or even a believer has come to terms with God through his Holy Spirit. Yes we are to introduce those that are hungry for the Spirit of God to God but in doing so God has reassured us as well, that he is at work in these souls. I am as moved as the other person because I see Gods work in action. We should not depend on physical vision, feelings or our hearing to experience him, yes we have an invisible God but that doesn't mean he is not here with us, you cannot have words without action. We have God here in spirit and he was also here in the Flesh as our Savior Jesus Christ and now we have God as the Holy Spirit and in this our eyes, our "Spiritual eyes and ears of our soul, have been opened to us as Christ said they would be.

There are reasons why God came into this world. One, He loves us, we are his creation. Only He could save his creation, by bringing us the truth and showing his love. He had to create that path of the Holy Spirit to our souls so that he could dwell in us always.

Jesus celebrated the Passover with the Disciples in the Upper Room so that the whole world would know that the last and greatest sacrifice of the lamb was about to be repeated for a much bigger reason including the fact that He would be that lamb this time and instead of just saving the physical bodies of the first born before Moses took the Jewish people from Egypt, this sacrifice gives the opportunity to save everyone who believes in him and what he did to take away our sins, and just as it says in John 3:16 NIV 16. For God so loved the world that he gave his one and only Son, that whoever believes in him shall not perish but have eternal life.

"IT IS GOD I PRESUME"

How can anyone say we cannot believe in an unseen God when there are so many ways that we do see him? We, the followers of Jesus Christ cannot credit anyone else but God, our creator. Science tries to claim it, common sense is an excuse and there are no coincidences when you put it to the test. These two words came to mind the other day "Presumption" and "Perception—these are used a lot in our language their meanings are simply this: Presumption—when you are forming an opinion before seeing the facts, object, idea etc. and Perception—when you form an opinion, when you see the object or facts as they appear.

In the sermon and in some of our lessons, that we read at home, we have talked about what we see and what we cannot see "Physically". We have used phrases in our history that point that out, such as "don't shoot until you see the whites of their eyes," or seeing is believing, and as Thomas in the upper room in.

John 20:25 NIV 25. So the other disciples told him, "We have seen the Lord!" But he said to them, unless I see the nail marks in his hands and put my finger where the nails were, and put my hand into his side, I will not believe."

Perception includes the five senses; touch, sight, sound, smell, and taste "You can't give me physical proof that he exists, therefore, I can't believe in him. The Holy Spirit broke the rules of coincidence, common sense and all the laws of science.

Matthew 27:51 NIV 51. At that moment the curtain of the temple was torn in two from top to bottom. The earth shook, the rocks split.

Hebrews 10:19–21 NIV 19. Therefore, brothers and sisters, since we have confidence to enter the Most Holy Place by the blood of Jesus, 20. by a new and living way opened for us through the curtain, that is, his body, 21. and since we have a great priest over the house of God.

Then there was Pentecost in Acts 2:1–4 NIV 1. When the day of Pentecost came, they were all together in one place. 2. Suddenly a sound like the blowing of a violent wind came from heaven and filled the whole house where they were sitting. 3. They saw what seemed to be tongues of fire that separated and came to rest on each of them. 4. All of them were filled with the Holy Spirit and began to speak in other tongues as the Spirit enabled them.

John 20:29 NIV 29. Then Jesus told him, "Because you have seen me, you have believed; blessed are those who have not seen and yet have believed."

For us, "those that believe," there is no more skepticism. We are blessed and as followers we see as we follow Jesus the Christ today and forever, as for presumption it's a habit that needs to be taken out of our Dictionary's and "Google."

JUST NOT YOUR DAY OR JUST NOT YOUR LIFE

Standing at the Guard shack watching the workers come in early in the morning, I remembered those days on the production side of the plant, yea I was there once, but today the morning sun hadn't come up it wasn't even 0600 yet. I watched as friend I worked with a few years back get out of his car something fell out of his lunch bag, an apple or orange, something round that rolled, he picked it up, acting as if things were not working out right already, then I watched on as the rest of his lunch broke through the bag and all fell on the asphalt parking lot, (by the way, this wasn't my gate), I still had to leave to go to my gate, so the other guards were seeing the same thing I laughed in support and said "just isn't your day," and he said "now it ain't." Then after the last straw, we all said "Aaaah, just put it all back in the car and go back home," he laughed and said "that's what I ought to do."

Have you ever tried to do something that should have taken a couple minutes and it got serious and stupid and by the time you got done with it, you were not only frustrated but it actually took an hour or two instead of a minute or two? After reading the lessons we have had recently, the sermons of Jesus's Lineage, plus our daily lessons at home and from our Small group, leading up to the Birth of our Savior Jesus the Christ, I have been given the thought to put out

20

there the list of all the obstacle's that Jesus encountered as a Human being and why it had to be this way. Sort of, "the bag with the holes in it," if you refer to the story at the beginning. So now we know the Lineage of Jesus from Matthew 1:1–17 definitely not what you would think when David's name comes up. Jesus did miraculous things in his life, 37 miracles just named in the Bible. Everything from giving sight to the blind to raising people from the dead; feeding 5,000 with only five loaves and two fishes. All these miracles and people still fought off the thought that this could be the man they were waiting for from prophecy within their own texts written in the scrolls of their forefathers. I really do not need to list everything because the Prophecy of Isaiah actually came into its truth just as he received it and proclaimed it from God. Isaiah started his ministry 740 years before Jesus was born and 2,758 years from today and no one could have described it better than what the Lord revealed to him, so read this and see for yourselves "NIV" Isaiah 53:1. Who has believed our message and to whom has the arm of the Lord been revealed? 2. He grew up before him like a tender shoot, and like a root out of dry ground. He had no beauty or majesty to attract us to him, nothing in his appearance that we should desire him. 3. He was despised and rejected by mankind, a man of suffering, and familiar with pain. Like one from whom people hide their faces he was despised, and we held him in low esteem. 4. Surely, he took up our pain and bore our suffering, yet we considered him punished by God, stricken by him, and afflicted. 5. But he was pierced for our transgressions, he was crushed for our iniquities; the punishment that brought us peace was on him, and by his wounds we are healed.

"He even speaks of our issues even today as he goes on in verse 6". We all, like sheep, have gone astray, each of us has turned to our own way; and the Lord has laid on him the iniquity of us all.

I couldn't describe it any more than that. I would sum all of this up this way, Jesus became human, to live a life in the worst conditions, tempted beyond any measure in the most desperate of times. His life proves to us all that, we as humans can follow in his footsteps of a sinless life because as flesh and blood he did so. He then, because we are all sinners, allowed those people that denied him as our Savior to be crucified for our some, but all of our sins for all time as well. So as NIV Bible" reads in John 3:16 says: 16. For God so loved the world that he gave his one and only Son, that whoever believes in him shall not perish but have eternal life.

PLATFORM

I heard the word "Platform" the other day on the radio. This person was in the Hospital for an illness and she said that she used that illness as a platform to witness to others that she met in the same situation and even to those caregivers who saw how alive she looked and acted while in a situation that people otherwise give up hope to. I got to thinking about that word Platform. I usually hear it used in a political manner such as, He or she is taking the Position of Senator or the Senatorial platform. This person had used it in a completely different way. This person said that her illness gave her a platform to witness with. She was what the Lord needed her to be for a lot of somebodies that needed to hear the word.

You know I have been feeling like we are going to have a spiritual revival soon and I am talking about a step up and stand on a soapbox with the words that just come over us from the Holy Spirit and people are drawn to hear it because they are hungry for Gods truth. It is a rare thing I feel will come into or during my lifetime.

I can relate to this person because about a year ago when I was stuck in the Hospital with my own issues for two weeks I was prodded and poked and given this med and that med, it seemed like they were looking for everything that could be wrong not just what I was in for, but while I was in there I asked for my Bible, PC so I could check Email and write the words that the Holy Spirit led me to and also books that I read. I got sleep deprovision because of all the treatments for my lungs at all hours of the night and day. I spoke a lot about God while I was in there but not near as much as I should have, but the nurses, assistants and doctors had to ask questions about your feelings, depression and do you have thoughts of suicide. The answer was always about the same. I still have our God and Jesus, why would I want to destroy what God has created.

Are you afraid of dying was a rare question but I always said I know where lam going and so as a friend told me in his dealing with that, "that means my job is over here and I am going to a better place no more pain or pills or work I'm fine with that." But imagine a platform that fits you where you are what stands out that would bring people to the Lord? How about something you regret in your past? What if you and I used that platform to bring people to the Lord? You already know what it's like to carry that burden around in yourself. You would not only feel better about sharing but you have come to terms with it now and at the same time you have reached out to someone going through the same things that you have. I can Hear Paul's words ring out two verses come to mind:

1 Cor. 9:22–22. NIV 9. To the weak I became weak, to win the weak. I have become all things to all people so that by all possible means I might save some.

2 Cor. 12:7–10 7. NIV 7. or because of these surpassingly great revelations. Therefore, in order to keep me from becoming conceited, I was given a thorn in my flesh, a messenger of Satan, to torment me. 8. Three times I pleaded with the Lord to take it away from me…. 9. But He said to me, "My grace is sufficient for you, for my power is perfected in weakness." Therefore, I will boast all the more gladly in my weaknesses, so that the power of Christ may rest on me. 10. That is why, for the sake of Christ, I delight in weaknesses, in insults, in hardships, in persecutions, in difficulties For when I am weak, then I am strong….

So you see the mistakes you have made and asked forgiveness for, God will use to glorify his name by helping others through you.

"PRUNNING"

In the 1970's, Arthur Burns was a Jewish economist who had quite a solid reputation. He was on advisor to presidents, and wielded considerable influence in the Nation's Capital. From 1970 to 1978 he was the chairperson of the Federal Reserve. Once, Mr. Burns was asked to pray at a gathering of evangelical politicians. Quite frankly, nobody knew what kind of prayer this Jewish economist would come up with. Burns surprised everybody by slowly beginning this way: "Lord, I pray the Jews would come to know Jesus Christ." He paused for a second to let his words sink in. He began again: "And I pray that Buddhists would come to know Jesus Christ." People looked at each other across their tables. Burns began again, "And I pray that Muslims would come to know Jesus Christ." And then, most shocking of all, Burns said "And Lord, I pray that Christians would come to know Jesus Christ. (An article from the Lutheran Hour) and a fact check *(Os Guinness, The Call, Finding and Fulfilling the Central Purpose of Your Life (Nashville: Word Publishing, 1998), 106.)*

It makes me wonder about who we vote for and listen too, I've pretty much given up paying any attention to politics and what is going on in the White house. I want to call it the "Whitewashed house" and I think of the words Jesus Christ used to describe the pharisee's, and their actions in Matt. 23:27–28 NIV 27. "Woe to you, teachers of the law and Pharisees, you hypocrites! You are like whitewashed tombs, which look beautiful on the outside but on the inside are full of the bones of the dead and everything unclean. 28. In

25

the same way, on the outside you appear to people as righteous but on the inside, you are full of hypocrisy and wickedness.

It seems in many cases to have not changed. Oh, I see the issues that we should be concerned about and I see what we should be feeling strongly about and what we should just ignore, and biblically too. But one side pleading and the other disagreeing; it just seems like someone pulled the play board out from under the game and let the marbles scatter all over the table and onto the floor.

We can huff and puff all we want to but as I heard on K Love this morning, "why is it so hard to just give it to the Lord?" I would imagine our blood pressure would come down, our frustrated eating habits would go away and our family values would skyrocket. We would have more time to do the things our Lord is trying to get us to prepare for. In the prayer room this Saturday, we brought up a subject that should actually scare us to death.

A scripture that should be PLANTED vividly in our hearts and minds. "John 15:2 NIV" 2. He cuts off every branch in me that bears no fruit, while every branch that does bear fruit he prunes[a] so that it will be even more fruitful. So what branches do you think the Lord will take from you and Me next? Are we producing fruit for the Lord?

STAR TREK?
I DON'T THINK SO

I am a real crazy fan of star trek, but there is a story in the Bible that would make the Trekkie think twice about the transporter.

Acts 8:26–40 NIV Philip and the Ethiopian

26. Now an angel of the Lord said to Philip, "Go south to the road—the desert road—that goes down from Jerusalem to Gaza." 27. So he started out, and on his way he met an Ethiopian eunuch, an important official in charge of all the treasury of the Kandake (which means "queen of the Ethiopians"). This man had gone to Jerusalem to worship, 28. and on his way home was sitting in his chariot reading the Book of Isaiah the prophet. 29. The Spirit told Philip, "Go to that chariot and stay near it."

30. Then Philip ran up to the chariot and heard the man reading Isaiah the prophet. "Do you understand what you are reading?" Philip asked.

31. "Can I," he said, "unless someone explains it to me?" So he invited Philip to come up and sit with him.

32. This is the passage of Scripture the eunuch was reading: "He was led like a sheep to the slaughter, and as a lamb before its shearer is silent, so he did not open his mouth. 33. In his humiliation he was

deprived of justice. Who can speak of his descendants? For his life was taken from the earth."

34. The eunuch asked Philip, "Tell me, please, who is the prophet talking about, himself or someone else?" 35. Then Philip began with that very passage of Scripture and told him the good news about Jesus. 36. As they traveled along the road, they came to some water and the eunuch said, "Look, here is water. What can stand in the way of my being baptized?" [37] 38. And he gave orders to stop the chariot. Then both Philip and the eunuch went down into the water and Philip baptized him. 39. When they came up out of the water, the Spirit of the Lord suddenly took Philip away, and the eunuch did not see him again, but went on his way rejoicing. 40. Philip, however, appeared at Azotus and traveled about, preaching the gospel in all the towns until he reached Caesarea.

God can do all things he doesn't need a transporter as you can see If you are really lead by our Lord and Savior and he wants you somewhere to fulfill his purpose he will "make it so" He is not Jean Luke Picard or Captain Kirk, and he doesn't need a transporter to put anyone anywhere at any time, He is our God the great I AM.

TEN PERCENT A FRACTION OR A NUMBER

Do you Tithe? Tithe is a tenth that is a fact, it is also Old Testament teaching. Offering on the other hand is what we call our giving today that is what we call giving in the New Testament. This has proven to me, to be the same meaning given the changes of what we are to do with our offering. I feel that a tenth is small potatoes, but it is a starting point none the less.

It is the question that Haunts people in the building we call the Church which is a misrepresentation of words but it serves a purpose as the meeting place for "Church" which are the people. Whatever it is Tithe or offering it doesn't matter because the minute the subject is brought up, nervousness and Conviction rear they're ugly heads and soon there seems to be a mad dash for the door by some. After that rumor, insult, and rejection take they're place. Why you might ask? Because we know what is right, never mind all the explanation and excuses and I guess at some point, we must be a little greedy.

I have been reading a book by Mark Batterson called "All In." **In there was a story about John Wesley founder of the Methodist Church. In 1731 he made a covenant with God, he limited his expenses to an income ceiling of 28 pounds. The first year he made 30 so he gave 2. The next year it doubled so he gave 32 because he kept living on just the 28. The third year his income tripled to 90 and he still kept his expenses flat. His goal was to give away everything over that 28 pound that was what he used for bills and family needs. He never carried more than 100 pounds in his possession because he was afraid of storing up earthly treasure. He believed that Gods blessings should result in us not raising our standard of living, but our standard of giving. He gave away within his lifetime approximately 30,000 pounds, adjusting for inflation.

Try to wrap your mind around this for just a little bit. The preacher gets up to gives a sermon the word "tithing" comes up, oh no, here we go again, can't we just hear the sermon, without him speaking about money? "Again" isn't it bad enough we see the plate go around every Saturday and Sunday without having to hear about it too.

Malachi 3:10 mentions tithing: NIV 10. Bring the whole tithe into the storehouse, that there may be food in my house. Test me in this," says the Lord Almighty, "and see if I will not throw open the floodgates of heaven and pour out so much blessing that there will not be room enough to store it.

Jesus said it best when he spoke of the woman and the two mites In Mark 12:41–44 41. Jesus sat down opposite the place where the offerings were put and watched the crowd putting their money into the temple treasury. Many rich people threw in large amounts. 42. But a poor widow came and put in two very small copper coins, worth only a few cents.

43. Calling his disciples to him, Jesus said, "Truly I tell you, this poor widow has put more into the treasury than all the others. 44. They all gave out of their wealth; but she, out of her poverty, put in everything—all she had to live on."

Then read Matthew 26:7 or 2 Corinthians 9:6–8 we already know the Lord "needs" nothing from us:

Psalms 50:10 NIV for every animal of the forest is mine, and the cattle on a thousand hills and, Matthew 6:8 NIV 8. Do not be like them, for your Father knows what you need before you ask him.

THE WAY A MECHANIC UNDERSTANDS GOD

I have said it before and I will say it again: When some go to the wrecking yard they see junk and something on its way to the crusher.

When I see a car at the wrecking yard all mangled, I see endless possibilities. I see wheels for a car to move on, a steering system to turn the car, an engine to move the car and etc, etc, etc.

Like the surgeon that see's a good heart for a dying patient or a kidney to save a young child's life. So these are our Masterpiece's.

The Lord looks on us with loving eyes on the heart and see's us as his children that he has always loved. God has endless opportunities for us, we are His masterpieces. Rom. 12:5. NIV. so in Christ we, though many, form one body… is with Christ's body. We are many parts of one body… and we all belong to each other.

This is the reason I write these analogies, so it will draw others to the scriptures, I write of these that apply to my life and for any that need to understand this in your lives.

Like the parts of the Body that are physical a Doctor has studied the way they work and learns the movements and the reason for all those parts in order to fix them, a Mechanic studies the workings of all parts of a vehicle so that he can fix it. God knows the Human body because he created it This surpasses all understanding because he is all knowing God is the great I Am.

TODAY'S HERO'S FOR GOD

You know, as followers of Christ, we find those morsels in Hollywood that sanctify our relationship with God. In life we seek Gods seeks Truth and sometimes, just sometimes Hollywood gets a script of Gods truth and puts it on the silver screen. It touches and moves hearts and even souls. I am inspired once again by the true history in theater. There are three that stand out, but today I watched "Hacksaw Ridge" again about the conscientious objector Desmond Doss. The best truth in action of God, in these times. The other two are "Sargent York" and another WWII Movie called, "The Great Zamperini." These are more prevalent to me I guess because I was in the military. For anyone else it would be difficult to watch and realize that the realism in war "is this real." The carnage and death shown was so authentic it would turn a lot of people's stomachs and a few of us that even knew what it was and is.

I believe that anyone in the military at one time or another has been touched in one way or another by God. We may set it aside for a distance of time, we may not want to go back to those things that may bother us or hasn't yet, but if and when you revisit it again, 'and you really should no matter how much pain that it takes. You will see places, people and things that stand out and that you will or cannot explain.

Chew on that moment, study your Bible on these moments and God will reveal himself to you, like me you will then understand what and why you were there. We are all Gods Hero's whether we come from a colorful past, a past we once believed in or we followed Gods way all of our lives. "IT DOESN'T MATTER, what matters is the outcome of God in your life and the lives of those that you share Him with, "your story will touch someone's life if you give it to God."

TRIPS TO THE BURNING BARREL

When I was a boy growing up in Ohio, we had a burning barrel. I had to take the trash out and burn it once a week. The idea of getting rid of trash is when it builds up you will be out there for a while your too afraid to walk away from it because the dry grass from mowing could start a brush fire especially in the summer. You don't leave it unattended. Just like sin you don't want to let it build up, you need to face it and give it to the Lord and ask forgiveness as soon as possible, you don't want to live with that burden all your life, you don't want it to build up either!

Who do you or who can you ever tell those silent secrets too? There is only one that can give a time and place to hear your problems of the day, only one is ever present to hear your grief, your secrets or the sin which you hold in that secret place in your heart where mold and rot grows and pierces even to your mind and twists in your gut. You do not have to live with that kind of turmoil. You and I have longed for someone we can trust or someone that would just listen to us about that thing we have held such hatred of self for!

God is waiting for you to give it to him. Believe in him, that he will take that admission of guilt to a place you cannot find; as far as the East is from the West! There is no measurement for that length, you cannot fathom it, you cannot wrap your mind around it but

God loves you that much. Psalms 103:11–13. NIV "11. For as high as the heavens are above the earth, so great is his love for those who fear him; 12. As far as the east is from the west, so far has he remove our transgressions from us. 13. As a father has compassion on his children, so the LORD has compassion on those who fear him;"

Learn from this and from all of his words, thank him for his forgiveness always and for the sacrifice His Son Jesus Christ made on the cross on Calvary. As the trash/sin builds up it must be taken on that walk to your knees in prayer to God through Jesus Christ with the help of the Holy Spirit or it will get deeper and deeper. Remember how it felt once you were relieved of that sin before and do not repeat, but look to Him that set you free. 1 Corinthians 10:13:13. NIV No temptation has overtaken you except what is common to mankind. And God is faithful; he will not let you be tempted beyond what you can bear. But when you are tempted, he will also provide a way out so that you can endure it.

WE ARE THE ROCKS WILL WE CRY OUT?

When something touches us deeply do we turn our heads? Yes, some do, until it hits the home front. What do we do when something unimaginable happens to you or to a family member or a close friend? Do we turn our heads? I just read a sobering story about something that happened last year and yes things like this have happened before, but this was a breath-taking situation and not in a good way.

The internet can do marvelous things and a lot of bad things as well, but this was neither and more! On Sept 2nd 2015 a little boy washed up on shore he was only three years old. Now, reading this is easier on the eyes than seeing it, so when I say "sobering" I mean it in the way it is perceived, It means" if I was stone drunk, I would become instantly sober at the sight of this picture". That is where the internet comes in. When you are curious these days you don't look in the papers anymore or a microfiche, you Google it, right? That is where I saw a fully dressed three-year-old boy laying on a beach. At first sight, it just looked like he was sleeping in the sand with his clothes on; now, knowing the story about this beautiful Syrian boy named Aylan Kurdi, his brother and mother have come to life in me. The War-torn Country of Syria, has been devastated even to the point of escaping it So if I was the one that discovered this young boy and I had to take a picture of it I would really be tempted to put my camera down and never pick it up again.

When refugees from this country try to get other countries attention about a problem I would imagine it gets sidelined, but when you see the devastation and a picture of a small boy dead in the sand washed up on a beach I think of the scripture Luke 19:39–41 NIV. 39 Some of the Pharisees in the crowd said to Jesus, "Teacher, rebuke your disciples!"

40. "I tell you," He replied, "If they keep quiet, the stones will cry out"

41. As he approached Jerusalem and saw the city, he wept over it.

So what now? How many of you want to go home or go see your kids and grandbabies this very second? Better yet, how many are looking at all the children and people in a different way? Do you think Jesus look at all of his children the same? I believe he does. He cares about the sick, the needy, the lost, the rich and the diseased. When I see devastation like this it makes me want to cry out like those proverbial rocks that Jesus talked about.

Can you imagine being at the edge of a discovery and being told you can't say a word and you have to leave? What would you do if a person would not heed your warning about something about to happen to them and just walk right into it? Would you watch and not try to prevent? I think this is what Jesus was trying to say.

So what do we do now? I think we should listen more and talk less, but be prepared to cry out like those rocks. Have you ever said; "That room just screams" fix me up" or that car is yelling, "wash me." Jesus said you can't shut me up if you did the rocks themselves would cry out. We need to live like that! When will you make your case for Christ? Have you already? Is the Holy Spirit telling you to cry out when you see something so vivid as this? God Bless you all who are standing up for our Christ. He loves and wants us all and he is coming back.

WE SHOULD BE PRAISING OUR LORD MORE....

While some of our lives have the good things, a husband, wife, boy-friend, girlfriend, Kids and Grandkids Some of us are stuck with things like regret, anguish and fear What we don't see is with God those good things can and will get better. With the regret, anguish and fears; we need to first give it all to the Lord so that we can move on His grace will bless you and you will be able to move on and by doing so, the gifts that he will give you along with listening for his Holy Spirits promptings, will continue to bless you if you follow where they lead you. It will turn your life into a blessing both to you and to those you share Him with around you.

2 Cor, 72:9 NIV. 9 But he said to me, "My grace is sufficient for you, for my power is made perfect in weakness" Therefore, I will boast all the more gladly about my weaknesses, so that Christ's power may rest on me. So instead of worrying about tomorrow let God worry about it Give it to him and prepare to be amazed by the works he is about to give you and you will share with others for him. Matt. 6:34 NIV. 34 Therefore do not worry about tomorrow, for tomorrow will worry about itself. Each day has enough trouble of its own.

WHAT LIVES REALLY MATTER

In the midst of a War, or a ship that is about to sink; or when a plane is about to crash or there's violence and turmoil in the streets, what lives really matter? When tragedy strikes like the storms of the sea or the fires that don't burn out in the western woods, the hurricanes, tornadoes, floods or drought, do all lives matter? Do we take time to choose who will survive? I don't see it that way, I refuse to look at it that way. That isn't the way I was brought up, that's not what my God Wants.

Romans 5:6–7 NIV 6. You see, at just the right time, when we were still powerless, Christ died for the ungodly. 7. Very rarely will anyone die for a righteous person, though for a good person someone might possibly dare to die. Whose eyes do we look through? What do we choose to see, what do we choose not to see? Do we look at color, race, or gender?

1 Samuel 16:7 NIV 7. But the Lord said to Samuel, "Do not consider his appearance or his height, for I have rejected him. The Lord does not look at the things people look at. People look at the outward appearance, but the Lord looks at the heart. "If a young child or an infant is in the path of a speeding car, ls the word racism a subject that would mingle in your mind? Do you decide to act on or simply walk away and not get involved? If you see someone being beaten, robbed or raped, do you walk away or around?

Matt. 25:34–40. 34. Then the King will say to those on his right, 'Come, you who are blessed by my Father; take your inheritance, the kingdom prepared for you since the creation of the world. For I was hungry and you gave me something to eat, I was thirsty and you gave me something to drink, I was a stranger and you invited me in, 36. I needed clothes and you clothed me, I was sick and you looked after me, I was in prison and you came to visit me.'

37. Then the righteous will answer him, 'Lord, when did we see you hungry and feed you, or thirsty and give you something to drink? 38. When did we see you a stranger and invite you in, or needing clothes and clothe you? 39. When did we see you sick or in prison and go to visit you?'

40. "The King will reply, 'Truly I tell you, whatever you did for one of the least of these brothers and sisters of mine, you did for me.

Have things gone SO wrong that there is no right?

If we care for the young no matter what color, race, gender or nationality ask yourself that tough question; "What Changed"? When did we change and why? Was it opinions, the Media, or the way you were raised? Matt. 19:13–14 NIV 13. Then people brought little children to Jesus for him to place his hands on them and pray for them. But the disciples rebuked them.

14. Jesus said, "Let the little children come to me, and do not hinder them, for the kingdom of heaven belongs to such as these."

When I was in the service there was no color, no nationality, and no racism! We were there for one common goal we learned to get along, we developed words like buddy, friend, brother and sister, and it was family! So, tell me isn't that what Jesus taught us? Love is not a bad word it's the only word that matters, if we don't Love one another what is left Romans 5:8 NIV 8. But God demonstrates His own love for us in this: While we were still sinners, Christ died for us.

So, I leave you with this to Ponder Feed on these words and not on Hate Look at life from that perspective that our creator gave us. Why wouldn't you call it the "Greatest Commandment."... Matt. 22:37–39 NIV 37. Jesus replied: "'Love the Lord your God with all your heart and with all your soul and with all your mind.' 38. This is the first and greatest commandment. 39. And the second is like it: 'Love your neighbor as yourself.'

"Let Me Make A Difference Father"

What is really important

I saw this and I felt the need to read Mark 8:36 KJV and the thoughts led to this: And on the back wall of that church was an inscription that changed my life forever. It said:

"For what profits a man if he shall gain the whole world and lose his own soul?" If I had won that senate race, I might well have gone on to "gain the whole world" and lost my own soul" By Michael Huffington 2008.

With this we all need to ask ourselves, to what is "that" important to me? The only answer with all popularity, fame and money hanging in the balance of life is, what is next? Wouldn't Life after death and unconditional love be more rewarding! We no longer have to sacrifice anything, because of one man that has already done what we could not, for all sin then, now and for all. We know him as Jesus Christ and the answer would be "NOTHING in all this world"

What were the disciples doing right before Jesus left for the last time?

They were fishing! They didn't remember what he told them from the beginning. He linked their earthly job in words to explain what they needed to do now. They were still fisherman but now they are fishers of men. Man does not live on bread alone remember that statement! Matt. 4:4 NIV 4. But Jesus answered, "It is written: 'Man shall not live on bread alone, but on every word that comes from the mouth of God.'"

That my friend is where we need to be. Memories of a world that passes us by is not the spiritual heaven that will always be, that we have been freely given. Because of that memory of His dying on the Cross for our sins which we need to give to him. Our hunger to read, learn and savor the scriptures will ever be in us. Matt. 28:19–20 NIV 19. Therefore, go and make disciples of all nations, baptizing them in the name of the Father, and of the Son, and of the Holy Spirit,

20. And teaching them to obey everything I have commanded you. And surely I am with you always, to the very end of the age." This is the great Commission.

WHAT IS REALLY IMPORTANT

I saw this and I felt the need to read Mark 8:36 KJV and the thoughts led to this: And on the back wall of that church was an inscription that changed my life forever. It said:

"For what profits a man if he shall gain the whole world and lose his own soul?" If I had won that senate race, I might well have gone on to "gain the whole world" and lost my own soul" By Michael Huffington 2008.

With this we all need to ask ourselves, to what is "that" important to me? The only answer with all popularity, fame and money hanging in the balance of life is, what is next? Wouldn't Life after death and unconditional love be more rewarding! We no longer have to sacrifice anything, because of one man that has already done what we could not, for all sin then, now and for all. We know him as Jesus Christ and the answer would be "NOTHING in all this world."

WHAT WERE THE DISCIPLES DOING RIGHT BEFORE JESUS LEFT FOR THE LAST TIME?

They were fishing! They didn't remember what he told them from the beginning. He linked their earthly job in words to explain what they needed to do now. They were still fisherman but now they are fishers of men. Man does not live on bread alone remember that statement! Matt. 4:4 NIV 4. But Jesus answered, "It is written: 'Man shall not live on bread alone, but on every word that comes from the mouth of God.'"

That my friend is where we need to be. Memories of a world that passes us by is not the spiritual heaven that will always be, that we have been freely given. Because of that memory of His dying on the Cross for our sins which we need to give to him. Our hunger to read, learn and savor the scriptures will ever be in us. Matt. 28:19–20 NIV 19. Therefore, go and make disciples of all nations, baptizing them in the name of the Father, and of the Son, and of the Holy Spirit, 20. And teaching them to obey everything I have commanded you. And surely I am with you always, to the very end of the age." This is the great Commission.

PART 2

GOD'S PROTECTION

BACK SLIDING

I saw this word mentioned on Facebook and I especially understand how this person worded the falling away or what some would call getting lost in the world or the infamous words "Back sliding".

Some actually think that once they have gone there, to the more worldly ways, that their sin is greater than Jesus Christs sacrifice. "Running from God to the world," is a perfect explanation of those terms that we try to describe how fallen we get in those rough times in our lives that we cannot handle.

Point A to Point B is a popular way of explaining our destination these days but when you're a Born Again follower of Jesus Christ, both A and point B are the same destiny. You cannot run far enough and leave Him, for He is standing at both ends with open arms.

Psalms 139 is so perfect to read during our struggle: 139:7–12 NIV

7   Where can I go from your Spirit?
    Where can I flee from your presence?
8   If I go up to the heavens, you are there;
    if I make my bed in the depths, you are there.
9   If I rise on the wings of the dawn,
    if I settle on the far side of the sea,
10 even there your hand will guide me,
    your right hand will hold me fast.

11 If I say, "Surely the darkness will hide me
and the light become night around me,"
12 even the darkness will not be dark to you;
the night will shine like the day,
for darkness is as light to you.

What part of this psalms describes where you feel you are at?
Does this comfort you?

The disciples did not grasp the fact that Jesus would eventually die on a Cross and be raised from the dead for all our sins, even knowing what the prophet Isaiah said in chapter 53 about the coming savior so long ago!

Did you or have you forgotten the promise of John 3:16 NIV for God so loved the world that He gave his one and only Son, that whoever believes in him shall not perish but have eternal life?

What are you putting first in your life that you cannot see this promise over all the worldly things?

There is nothing this world offers that is more important than your eternity. He wants you to walk with Him, confide in him, but most of all He wants you to love him as unconditionally as He loves you. Gods Promise never changed and it will never change.

YFICA

DO OR DIE

I have to vent a little, I have been confused about some of the protests and the news of tragedy that has been taking place in schools lately. I cannot rap my brain around this world's loss of and thought about children.

What is going on? I am in tears trying to figure out who I do not want to offend and who to mourn for.

A news broadcast about several different shootings in public schools versus protests all over the world over the rights of women to have abortions.

We are debating whether to abort or kill an Embryo from time of inception up to the day of birth and at the same time we talk about preventing suicide in this world and now they want to vote on one of the very reasons that some women take their own lives, in regret of what they have decided earlier in their own lives and worse yet there are the ones that want a child and end up having a miscarriage wondering why they could not deliver a child naturally.

I do not hate anyone! Whatever the decision or issue that has happened about all of this, even if I do not agree with it, I always say Hate the sin not the sinner and we are all sinners, but those things that are happening are still confusing. I think that our real enemy is the devil himself and his demons and I refuse to allow him to drag me into his trap.

1 Peter 5:8 NIV 8. Be alert and of sober mind. Your enemy the devil prowls around like a roaring lion looking for someone to devour.

Through all of this I am hanging on to those two greatest commands that Jesus reminded us in scripture <u>Mark Chapter 12:28–31 NIV</u>

<u>28 One of the teachers of the law came and heard them debating. Noticing that Jesus had given them a good answer, he asked him, "Of all the commandments, which is the most important?"</u>
<u>29 "The most important one," answered Jesus, "is this: 'Hear, O Israel: The Lord our God, the Lord is one. 30 Love the Lord your God with all your heart and with all your soul and with all your mind and with all your strength.' 31 The second is this: 'Love your neighbor as yourself.' There is no commandment greater than these."</u>

There are no if's and's or but's about it! What he said takes in every situation and everyone who sins against Him, their brother, sister or family members or even our own enemy's? That takes in even these people that make these decisions.

I will not allow the evil to drag me low when so many are lost, Jesus gave us the perfect example of how we are to love one another as we love ourselves.

GOD IS "I AM," SYNONYMOUS TO INFINITY

When Moses was with God on the Mountain of God "Horeb" in Exodus 3:13–14 NIV 13. And Moses said unto God, Behold, when I come unto the children of Israel, and shall say unto them, The God of your fathers hath sent me unto you; and they shall say to me, what is his name? What shall I say unto them?

14. And God said unto Moses, I Am That I Am: and he said, thus shalt thou say unto the children of Israel, I Am hath sent me unto you.

Have you ever really thought about that answer? It is so perfect an answer that no one, I mean no one can elaborate, add to or take away from it!!!! Have you ever looked into what they call an" infinity mirror." It is an allusion but this definition goes on forever. It is like a math problem you never reach a final answer for, it just continually goes on and on.

There is another perfect answer that includes us, if we believe in God and I do, these are some of the reasons why God the Son and the Holy Spirit are the trinity. The one who died on the cross for our sins is that part of God that is flesh "that is real too!" Psalms 103:12 NIV "As far as the east is from the west, so far hath he removed our transgressions from us."

I guess whoever came up with Buzz light-year was right in his word "To Infinity and Beyond" YFICA

GROWING UP

I have been taught that sin is not to be done, that one sin is just as bad as another and we all do it anyways. So, I read this:

Matthew 12:31–32 (NIV)

31. And so I tell you, every kind of sin and slander can be forgiven, but blasphemy against the Spirit will not be forgiven. 32. Anyone who speaks a word against the Son of Man will be forgiven, but anyone who speaks against the Holy Spirit will not be forgiven, either in this age or in the age to come.

If it starts to bother you or you are having guilty feelings, it is coming from the Holy Spirit! The Bible is "THE" Living Word of God. If you are fighting the conviction you are having from a sin, whether you think it is small or large, you are fighting against the inevitable, and 'you will somehow come to terms with it.' It will affect you physically, mentally and emotionally if you do not come clean.

The reason the Bible is called the living word is because whenever you read it, the Holy Spirit will speak through it to any person and it may be understood differently at any given time when it is read again. That same reading within any amount of time may change your thoughts in another way when you visit it again.

The Bottom Line is this: A 'sin is still a sin.' We should have all been brought up to know "right from wrong,"

If you believe in God, then you should believe in his word. "Was it written by man?" Yes, it was. God gave them what to write; From Moses of the books of Genesis and Exodus to John of Revelations on the isle of Patmos. These words are God breathed they serve us in any situation possible and through the Holy Spirit "judge" our actions and because of Jesus the Christ we believe and follow. If we stray, he will always forgive but sin will always be a sin and we all sin and fall short of the Glory of God. Whatever the sin is; arguing about it accomplishes nothing. It is between you and the Trinity, "God the Father, Jesus Christ the son and the breath and very spirit and words of God the Holy Spirit.

Romans 3:23–24 (NIV)

23 for all have sinned and fall short of the glory of God, 24 and all are justified freely by his grace through the redemption that came by Christ Jesus.

The answer to all of the bickering in this world has been summed up with the greatest commandment,

Mark 12:29–31 29 "The most important one," answered Jesus, "is this: 'Hear, O Israel: The Lord our God, the Lord is one. 30 Love the Lord your God with all your heart and with all your soul and with all your mind and with all your strength.'

31 The second is this: 'Love your neighbor as yourself.'[c] There is no commandment greater than these."

Questions:

Were you brought up knowing right from wrong?

What does it feel like when you do wrong? Do you ignore it or does it bother you?

HERE KITTY KITTY

I think the Lord was showing me something in our little pet Kitten! Last night and early this morning I thought about how I keep trying to dodge scratch marks from our little kitten, he's a real energetic piece of work. I try to calm him down and play nice by holding him tight enough that I can pet him and talk to him quietly. It doesn't work, he just wants to play, I can't seem to even tire him out. You know what they say about young snakes and scorpions, they are the most dangerous, because they cannot control their venom; well Kittens in the same way cannot and will not control their bites and scratching no matter how sharp those new claws and teeth are. It also makes me wonder what song would come out of our table cloth if we wrapped. It on a roll and put it in an old player piano.

In getting caught up in the moment, I felt the Lord giving me an example, a message. In that very same way, how many times have we thought we could control ourselves? It could be drugs, alcohol, sexual immorality, or whatever. It could be ice cream, even eating too much. We know what it is, and we gave it up because our Lord convicts us through his Holy Spirit. Our conscience has now, that we are Born again, become a conviction. We know right from wrong, you know, that first bite Adam and Eve took when they first got that uh, oh oops, feeling in the garden. You try to get away from it, it's on the shelf in front of you and you're staring at it. You are watching TV and it shows up on every channel, every commercial; you go out with friends and you hear the vulgar talk; a lot of us through our Lord have stopped talking like that from our early life. What do we do, the thought, don't be rude, goes through your mind. Do we fall into that language again, laugh along with everyone else? It is blasphemy to our Lord. We know it's not funny, it literally "hurts to laugh," as it should So like that Cat it doesn't want to quit playing but then what else does a cat do all day long it isn't sinning, "it's a cat" for crying out loud. Now ask yourself this; do you pet the cat nicely and say nice kitty or do you fall into its trap and start playing along regardless of whether you get bit and scratched again and again? 1 Peter 5:8–11 NIV 8. Be alert and of sober mind. Your enemy the devil prowls around like a roaring lion looking for someone to devour. 9. Resist him, standing firm in the faith, because you know that the family of believers throughout the world is undergoing the same kind of sufferings. 10. And the God of all grace, who called you to his eternal glory in Christ, after you have suffered a little while, will himself restore you and make you strong, firm and steadfast. 11. To him be the power for ever and ever. Amen.

Now the cat is really innocent, "and in its own right," but the example is there for us too. I don't wear shorts in my own house anymore and I'm thinking of ways to lure him away from me when I am relaxing in my chair but that's what the Holy Spirit has taught me today. Is he speaking to you, write it down and then study on it, even the simplest of things can be a lesson from the Lord and that my brother and sister is the Holy Spirit. Until the next time.

HOLY SPIRIT BREATHE OF GOD

The Holy Spirit is like a small bird that whispers in your ear and sometimes he's like the roaring Lion. He pushes you like the small child that wants you to go somewhere with them or the raging river that throws you to the nearest coastline. He knows what you want to hear but never speaks it. He knows what you need to listen to and it is the voice of God you will hear. What you need, VS what you want,

The Line in the Song by Toby Mac is so strong in me about the line that has been drawn and when the Sinner and the Saint meet, that line slides behind and further to the back of the sinner, and its washed away like the tide pushing further in to pull you closer to God the Fathers love.

Sometimes when we listen, we see wealth in knowledge, as to what his plan is. Sometimes we are directed to redirect to a place we would never want to go, but the gift of listening is just that, a gift, and it strengthens us in the fact that God always hears, and always answers. He is ALIVE in me, in you. I use the word inspiration like water running out of a spilled cup, because it doesn't stay in me. The Lord has streamed words through us as a vessel that never empties.

When we choose not to listen to him because of doubt the story goes even longer. That's ok, because there is a purpose no matter whether it's a long one, or the short one. Sometimes it's long because eventually it will touch more people's lives. Sometimes it's just to get the attention of one. Conviction comes in all sizes, some will cut to the bone after years of hiding, or it can come or it immediately after your eyes are open to it. Listening is the key, facing it, and asking forgiveness is the answer. How does someone get your attention do they whisper? Are you listening, or ignoring? DO they yell, because you don't see that train wreck coming at you? Do you keep walking across the tracks because your mind is made up?

The Holy Spirit is the breath of God, and Jesus delivered it to us, in person. What was the instructions on the box? Turn it over what did it say? Are we letting those tiny whims, sit in idol or are we still waiting for the fuel to light those fiery tongues that were so powerful in the day they were brand new people when we accept Jesus into our hearts the Holy Spirit is Brand new in us. Sinning is the last thing that is supposed to be on our minds. Everything in our garage, in our minds, our buildings, our driveways, and in the store windows is no longer supposed to be a necessity. We go back to that one word that launches a thousand ships or a word that can cause a disaster for thousands of people with God we can save people, without we can slip into a coma to the rest of the World? Free will from the Lord is given to us to show that we will make the right choice into GODs Will.

LIVING FOR HIS INSPIRATION

A friend of mine mentioned to me that she felt that our prayer warriors were being attacked. With all the illnesses of our warriors and their families and friends of the prayer room including the ministry itself, it did seem like an epidemic.

I replied. Yes, we are and with the political rivalry, Satan has gained a foothold and led a lot of people into some dark places.

Not all Christians are as immune as they should be. Some are questioning our ethics, (should we side with this decision or rally for a something better)? Sometimes we get caught off guard. It is a neatly plotted out plan. That's the difference between our heavenly father and Satan, God loves us unconditionally and has our eternity ready for us for the asking because of Jesus's sacrifice for all our sin. The devil wants us to do what we want for ourselves and the world and never be content.

IN PERSPECTIVE

In reading the UPPER ROOM today something caught my eye, I remember as a child and as an adult, when you look out over your lawn, a lawn, or anyone's lawn. What do you see? The weeds or did you see the pretty flower in the grass.

I feel we need to take a second look at all of God's creation, the hidden beauty that a child sees in everything. As an adult some of us look for the weeds in the yard or the flaws in a person, there way of speaking, a deformity, or the hearsay and not the truth. We look at large animals attacking and eating another small or young or weak animal and then on the other hand we see the mothers of those animals giving birth, and nurturing their young.

We need to look at everything for the beauty in it and quit looking for the flaws. That is a different perspective that is the way of the little Children they will lead the way by teaching us. If we could just teach the world to sing in perfect harmony—let's just do it and quit talking about it.

Matthew 19:14 NIV

"Jesus said, Let the little children come to me, and do not hinder them, for the kingdom of heaven belongs to such as these."

IT'S A SIN

We should all know the word that describes what will keep us out of Heaven and from God. It's those three letters that spell "sin," right? So what if we could subtract one thing from our lives or from this world that would prevent all sin, what would it be, desire, want, greed, or would it be temptation? Yes I would say "temptation", would be the elimination of the very thing that brought sin into this world.

I grew up learning how to fix things, so as I read Gods word and write what he wants given to those he has intended it for, I begin to wonder what is this all about. If I can help fix some of the small problems of this world with a wrench a hammer and a pencil, what more does he want of me or what else can I do?

Everyone has a gift and a calling, everyone that belongs to the body of Christ that is. There are still those that have not heard the word, or His truth, those eyes of their souls remain closed until they are opened to the truth.

"If, and again I say if we could rid this world of sin, things would be better and we would be closer to getting into heaven! "Hang on there," I'm not saying it could happen. There is and has been only one way for that to happen and it has already been done by our Lord and Savior on the Cross over 2,000 years ago. Jesus came into this world to show us that, just like he took away affliction from man and woman such as the gift of sight to the blind, taken away disease in the blink of an eye and make the crippled walk again, he has taken our sins away, past, present and future for all time, we only have to admit to God that we believe that his son did indeed die on the cross for that reason," and ask him for forgiveness for our sins.

That isn't the end of the journey either, it is just the beginning. Shouldn't that make us love our God even more? He wants us to put everything into his hands and love him with all of our hearts, souls, and mind. It is the greatest commandment and you can read it in his word, Matt. 22:37–40 NIV 37. Jesus replied: "'Love the Lord your God with all your heart and with all your soul and with all your mind.' 38. This is the first and greatest commandment. 39. And the second is like it: 'Love your neighbor as yourself.' 40. All the Law and the Prophets hang on these two commandments."

No we could never do away with sin. We have all sinned and fall short, but knowing the key ingredients we can try a little harder to limit it even further by putting it where it belongs far away and behind us by first realizing that it is in fact Temptation from, "THE DEVIL" it is his tool and it is one that doesn't belong to the Follower of Jesus Christ. We need to throw that tool out of our tool bags! The devil came into the garden as a snake and introduced us to temptation, and it has plagued us ever since. Let's fight against it by first recognizing it and then turn it over to Jesus and let him keep the devil in his place, Defeated when Jesus rose from the dead on Easter morn.

INFLUENCED

Some of you might have heard this at your jobs if you ever had to deal with Hazardous Material. I thought it would be a good example of the Human Behavior we have all seen and dealt with in this world and may be dealing with in our own families. It was a short feature on how you handle contaminated waste in the work space.

The man explaining this was holding a glass of wine in his hand and he was holding it over a barrel of contaminated waste. Then he asked, "Now if I were to let a drop of this wine fall into this barrel I would still have a glass of drinkable Wine and this barrel would still be contaminated waste, right? But if I were to take a drop of this waste and put it into this wine then it would all be contaminated, wouldn't it?

This is the same way that "influence" works in prejudices, Alcohol, drugs, tobacco or anything that is seen as something that, "maybe just once won't hurt" or "we will fit into the crowd, if we try it just that once".

You are introduced into something that under normal circumstances you would never even think to do or try. You get excuses from people like: "Everybody else does it," or, "It hasn't messed me up."

Habits and influence can go a long way in all generations. You start thinking maybe my kids will pick up on this.

So being a grandfather I want to say something to you younger Parents out there; "Why wait until you start telling them they shouldn't, when you can teach them to say no and do the right things

62

from the get go. Know what to say to your children and grandchildren before they ask what those words mean or why is the world the way it is, or why is our country fighting all the time. We need to focus on what God has intended us to do and not to do, not what the world wants to influence us into doing and saying. Don't be that drop of waste in the tall glass of clean drinking water, be the one who serves the water to others uncontaminated to all others, John 4:14 NIV 14. But whoever drinks the water I give them will never thirst. Indeed, the water I give them will become in them a spring of water welling up to eternal life." not just your family, Gods family and that's everywhere and everyone.

There are good influences and bad, just like habits good and bad. Stop or break the bad habits, be a good influence to others.

Psalms 119:104–105 NIV 104. I gain understanding from your precepts; therefore I hate every wrong path. 105. Your word is a lamp for my feet, a light on my path.

IS THERE ANY ESCAPE

You cannot survive sin and climb out on top, it's a losing battle and the only way to get out is Jesus. Jesus Christ took the sins of this world upon himself, and came out on top. We can to, if we only believe in what he did, the sacrifice he made and why he did it and how it covered us for all time. John 3:16 16. For God so loved the world that he gave his one and only Son, that whoever believes in him shall not perish but have eternal life.

It was like our Fireroom aboard ship, it was the lowest place on the ship. If the ship sustained damage in those areas, the crew in those spaces, in order to save the most lives and keep the ship from sinking, had to shut and lock the hatches in a worst-case scenario. You had one chance to escape, but you had to finish the job you were trained to do, I was a do or /and die situation, was to first secure the boilers in the space, and then you would have to go to the lower level to something called the "escape Trunk." "If" you were able to get the door open you would be able to climb out to topside to at least one story up.

The trick is getting it open, it only opens one way and if there is too much water up against it you never will.

Surviving while going through sin to come out on top is a losing battle you could be at your lowest possible place in life and you see that door and you push and push but you just can't get it open, but in this case all you have to do is answer the knock and open that door. Luke 11:9–10 NIV 9. "So I say to you: Ask and it will be given to you; seek and you will find; knock and the door will be opened to you. 10. For everyone who asks receives; the one who seeks finds; and to the one who knocks, the door will be opened.

LUCIFER IS GRINNING ALL DAY AND EVERY DAY

We are warned, we've been told, and we live around it every minute of every day! This day and age to God, is like so many others that He has seen. It is a Deja vu moment for the I AM. We have never payed attention, to its slow, progressive, seeping of hate, immorality, and filth, yes, its name is sin.

Nowadays it starts out as "unknown", then they use the word "wicked" like it's supposed to be a cool thing. They don't even realize what they're saying or doing because it's so subtle. We are so desensitized over these things that we don't even flinch at a minor change much less a major change of decision in our laws, ways of life, or things unheard of not more than a couple of years ago! The devil is so ingenious we can't even say the littlest things without starting a hate that burns and grows in and around us like a forest fire.

Jesus said Love thy neighbor as thyself and the news media fuels more uncertainty as to who our neighbors are. We hear one thing and we say another. It's like Gods two-edged sword is being mocked by a two-faced mirror!

We see Leader's leading us down the wrong path and we continue to follow because some have been led to believe it's the right thing to do. But there are those of us that see it's not and try to stop the herd, but we get trampled into the dust. The rest are just sheep being pushed over the edge quietly and gently as to not spook the ones that are in line to an oblivion.

We all need to look to the Lords words all the time; you can see how we got into this mess and why it is happening again and again. This is what the Bible is for; there are scary things in there, your right and it's repetitive too.

How many times do we have to get burned on the stove or touch the hot iron, or step on that loose board before we learn there are instructions on what to do to keep from repeating mistakes like this? I will say it again read the Bible! There are examples and what to do is in his word. Read it, look for your situation, you will find it!

The story of Adam and Eve and the first deadly sin. Noah was commissioned to save the human race with his family and all the animals in an Ark. Even then Noah, being a pure man after Gods own heart, got into a conversation on whether or not God should destroy them as well and so Noah and his family were spared to start a new story. Evil was destroyed over the whole earth, but the foothold was still there, Lucifer had to just start over.

Then there was Moses who saw Gods glory freed and led his people to the Promised Land after being in captivity under Pharaoh. Then there was Joshua and the battle of Jericho, and Elijah and Elisha etc. etc. This is only a few but God used them to clean up the mess that our ancestors made of the Human race this is not new news this is an ever-setting sun on the human race.

We never seem to learn but God still loves us and the only argument and saving grace we have is the love we can pour out to our Lord and Savior Jesus Christ in our Loving conversations in Prayer. We give Him our Faith that he will heal this land, His People, us! We need to speak to him fervently and Listen for his answers, pay attention to His Holy Spirit, and repeat as much as humanly possible. Don't stop Praying and if you don't already, start as soon as possible!

OUR FIRST LINE OF DEFENSE "THE ARMOR"

I think it is getting time to take those idols that get in the way and put them out of our houses, out of our lives, we've turned the TV into a necessity! Have you ever wondered what has been happening to our minds even our very souls, from watching that tube? It is a true, verifiable, addiction, it can literally be the worst addiction on this planet.

I try to watch a good wholesome show and when I do the devil slips a compromising commercial about our earthly behaviors and how to relax and lead it into sin and suggests that we be more relaxed in that behavior! It has made "immorality," (the state of being immoral; wickedness), into a challenge, the Devil is using it to twist our minds of that definition into a normal behavior that will ruin our Godly lives of right vs wrong into the opposite, which is the way of the world.

What a perfect plan, He is really up to date and getting better at it every minute of every day. He is up on electronics, Hollywood, and Politics, he has got his fingers in everything under the sun.

1 Peter 5:8–9 NIV 8. Be alert and of sober mind. Your enemy the devil prowls around like a roaring lion looking for someone to devour. 9. Resist him, standing firm in the faith, because you know that the family of believers throughout the world is undergoing the same kind of sufferings.

We are Human, but when we become followers of Christ and things get us down, we tend to look through a magnifying glass by way of human behavior. That is "our" human behavior. But we have forgotten to put on the New; the full Armor that Paul wrote about it.

Eph. 6:10–18 10. Finally, be strong in the Lord and in his mighty power. 11. put on the full armor of God, so that you can take your stand against the devil's schemes. 12. For our struggle is not against flesh and blood, but against the rulers, against the authorities, against the powers of this dark world and against the spiritual forces of evil in the heavenly realms. 13. Therefore put on the full armor of God, so that when the day of evil comes, you may be able to stand your ground, and after you have done everything, to stand. 14. Stand firm then, with the belt of truth buckled around your waist, with the breastplate of righteousness in place, 15. And with your feet fitted with the readiness that comes from the gospel of peace. 16. In addition to all this, take up the shield of faith, with which you can extinguish all the flaming arrows of the evil one. 17. Take the helmet of salvation and the sword of the Spirit, which is the word of God. 18. And pray in the Spirit on all occasions with all kinds of prayers and requests. With this in mind, be alert and always keep on praying for all the Lord's people.

1 Cor. 13:11–12 NIV states: 11. When I was a child, I talked like a child, I thought like a child, I reasoned like a child. When I became a man, I put the ways of childhood behind me. 12. For now we see only a reflection as in a mirror; then we shall see face to face. Now I know in part; then I shall know fully, even as I am fully known.

2 My point is this, our first line of defense is to talk to God and that is prayer any way you cut it, that is where we go first! All through our lives we have been told talk to your father, go to your supervisor, see your Commander, talk to your Boss, talk to your Wife or Husband. All through your life you have looked up to these for advice. We have been given orders and question what is next, what we do, how do I deal with this or that for direction. All of this, while our Lord stands in the background until we realize that there the first one we should turn to and take everything to is Jesus Christ God and the Holy Spirit they are one and the same.

When we hear rumors about the Church get on your knees, the election for a new leader, get on your knees, problems at home, on your knees, loss of a loved one part of you is part of him, on your knees, praises don't forget get on your knees. We are all Prayer warriors at one time or another, but we need to be Full time Prayer Warriors because it is our FIRST LINE OF DEFENSE against the devil and all his plans to fall into your human behavior. I struggle, we all struggle and while that will make us stronger for things to come we still need to live through it to see what God has in mind and what that strength is needed for, for his Glory.

I think its high time to kick him as far away as possible how can we be more like Christ if we stay "JUST" under the radar, Just out of range? It is time for "the Armor" we all know that needs to be put it on every day. We do not want it to get dusty! Be at the ready my brothers and Sisters we are headed for a Bumpy Ride!

PROBLEMS OR OPPORTUNITY...?

I don't think we go out looking for trouble, or create a problem but as we all know problems happen to us all None of us want problems or difficulties. We don't want to hear bad news or the mistakes we make or someone else's for that matter because it creates uncomfortable situations. We don't want to hear that a loved one is dying, has Cancer or even lose a family pet even though we know it is inevitable.

When that time comes or those rough moments come, we have a choice The worldly choice is to give up and stay recluse to yourself To you it feels like the beginning of the end, there are those who don't want to speak to anyone or even step outside their door. You are hurting and you just want to be left alone. You can give it to the Lord, you can always talk to him or a friend that can intercede for you in Prayer with and for you.

When this is done you should listen for Him to speak into your life and give you guidance and direction Frustrated? Yes, It can be, you see the Lord has a plan and it is all going to happen in his time not ours If there is one thing, I have learned it is that everything with God is an ongoing test If you take the easy road, you will not be able to learn what he has in store for you and it will be a long road to nowhere The other choice will seem and may be more difficult but it will be more rewarding because that's the one God has on "his agenda" for you. It is the participation in that race that Paul spoke of in Heb. 12:1 NIV 1 Therefore, since we are surrounded by such a great cloud of witnesses, let us throw off everything that hinders and the sin that so easily entangles And let us run with perseverance the race marked out for us.

Sometimes there is that special moment, or an act of random Kindness, or it is just something that you don't normally think to do For some reason our human minds cannot comprehend it. It is that knee jerk reaction, or that split second decision, an unplanned second thought. There is only one explanation and you can't deny it. It is all God; the Holy Spirit is moving in that very moment and it is always something your earthly self never expects. We need to live in Christ and be prepared for that moment, even though a lot of the times we won't see it coming. Trust in the Lord and he will give you direction for any situation. What is it that all of us that have known the Lord at one time or another, thinks of, the moment that we have hit rock bottom, the end of our rope or heard those words we never want to hear from a doctor. What seems to be the most important passage that we all need to speak, read or hear from someone or if only from our Lord himself in that time of trouble. To reach for that dusty Bible! I am guessing it's either the 23rd Psalms or the Lord's prayer we want to remember it, recite it. I am not a mind reader but I will guess that a lot of us have been there one time or another. So, when that time comes look it up or google it, if you cannot find it. Look to the walls of your mom's kitchen for the words on banners or your grammas plate that has those words on it. "Though I walk through the Valley of the Shadow of death;" and we will, some more than others and others only once.

Read what Paul said about running that race in Rom. 8:34–39 NIV

34. Who then is the one who condemns? No one. Christ Jesus who died—more than that, who was raised to life—is at the right hand of God and is also interceding for us.

35. Who shall separate us from the love of Christ? Shall trouble or hardship or persecution or famine or nakedness or danger or sword? 36. As it is written:

"For your sake we face death all day long; we are considered
as sheep to be slaughtered."

37. No, in all these things we are more than conquerors through
him who loved us. 38. For I am convinced that neither death nor
life, neither angels nor demons, neither the present nor the future,
nor any powers, 39. Neither height nor depth, nor anything else in
all creation, will be able to separate us from the love of God that is in
Christ Jesus our Lord.

So we have problems and our good Lord still gives us His unconditional love to create an opportunity to become stronger in Him
with the gifts he has given us. It is that AHA moment we cannot
afford to miss out on.

READING AND WRITING THOUGHTS AND REALITY

We all have a past and a glimpse of what "might" be ahead. I have known what God wants of me at times, and because of Free Will a lot of what I should not do, I did and I chose the wrong path at times. He spoke and I did not listen at times. He wanted me to but life, the earthly pressures, tempted me into those places I should not have gone, even at his warning.

1 Cor. 10:13 NIV 13. No temptation has overtaken you except what is common to mankind. And God is faithful; he will not let you be tempted beyond what you can bear. But when you are tempted, he will also provide a way out so that you can endure it. Everything on earth and Heaven has always been there.

Some know the Bible or at least the stories and history of sin. Some know it because we or another believer listened to you and the conversation showed you God, the only God that spoke before words were even a language and he sent his only son Jesus, who is the Flesh of those words and flesh of God on earth after Adam and Eve, who he loved first, because he created them first. Sin was then created from a temptation that we wish would not have been in the picture at all. It lured the sinless into a sinner in one bite and into what we all are now it also created death.

1 John 1–4, NIV 1. That which was from the beginning, which we have heard, which we have seen with our eyes, which we have looked at and our hands have touched—this we proclaim concerning the Word of life. 2. The life appeared; we have seen it and testify to it, and we proclaim to you the eternal life, which was with the Father and has appeared to us. 3. We proclaim to you what we have seen and heard, so that you also may have fellowship with us. And our fellowship is with the Father and with his Son, Jesus Christ. 4. We write this to make our joy complete. GOD, is "The Word" and spoke the word to the multitude to prepare them for the way to Eternity which is the only way to be where God wants you and wanted us all along in His loving arms as sinless and innocent as a baby or as a child. A few were given the Holy Spirit before, but Jesus gave us that Holy Spirit after he left this earth. You see the Holy Spirit is the breath of God "the word" and if we believe in what God in the flesh who is Jesus, and what he did by being tortured and dying on the cross for our sins we too may receive the Holy Spirit.

John 1:14 (NIV) 14. The Word became flesh and made his dwelling among us. We have seen his glory, the glory of the one and only Son, who came from the Father, full of grace and truth.

There has only been one man that has "never sinned" on this earth, Jesus who was tested and tried and died for those he came to save the sinner and the lost, the poor and the sick. He did not come to make the saved and pure of heart feel better, He came to show us, "the sinners," how to get to where he is now.

Luke 5:32 NIV 32. I have not come to call the righteous, but sinners to repentance." And then how to love our creator, our God and then our neighbors which is everyone who walks the face earth, so that they have the same opportunity to live in heaven with him. Jesus paid the rent on our mansions in heaven when he died on the cross. When he left this earth he even told the disciples he went to prepare a place for us.

John 3:16 (NIV) 16. For God so loved the world that he gave his one and only Son, that whoever believes in him shall not perish but have eternal life.

THE TIRED, THE POOR, THE HUDDLED MASSES

What if we looked at the lost, the poor, the hurting and the addicts, like we look at a drawer of files falling all over the place. On the floor, the desk, the table or the ground all mixed up. Like the wind blowing them all over the place and we run to stop them from all blowing away. What do we do about it? What do we do when we pick up all those papers those files or the basket of mixed clothes out of the dryer? I sometimes wonder if the Lord wants us to look at the problems and issues of this world like the mess that we have gotten it into. Well, if you're like me, I pick up and organize or try to put things back the way they were or better than they were. You know there's a place for everything and everybody God will see to it if you just ask.

We pick up all those papers and put them where they belong to, the laundry we sort out for example, Fred's socks and shirts and Wilma's dresses and hats they all have a place.

So if we can do this such a small scale in our own lives with our things papers clothes tools household items why wouldn't it work if everyone pitched in to take care of a larger problem? Jesus knew it is possible and everything is possible with Him.

Matt. 25:39–40 NIV 39. When did we see you sick or in prison and visit you? 40. And the King will reply, 'Truly I tell you, whatever you did for one of the least of these brothers of mine, you did for me.'

So when you see that person, you know a living breathing person, laying down on the sidewalk covered up with a cardboard box, think about that when you start sorting out your laundry and you cannot find that other sock, or you complain about dirt on that clean floor.

Duet. 15:11 NIV 11. There will always be poor people in the land. Therefore, I command you to be openhanded toward your fellow Israelites who are poor and needy in your land.

The sick and the lost, what did Jesus say about these.

Luke 5:31–32 NIV 31. Jesus answered, "It is not the healthy who need a doctor, but the sick. 32. I have not come to call the righteous, but sinners to repentance."

So what I am getting to is in a large scale WHAT IF we all picked up and helped with everything and everyone to get them to a better place and maybe, just maybe that is what Jesus was trying to get us to see!

He put every example in his book, the Bible, this is our manual, our instruction for a small or a large-scale problem. We are children of God / The Church/ the Body of Jesus Christ, we are the Physical Body with a Spiritual connection to God, through the Holy Spirit. When I see the lost, the broken, the hungry and the addicts I see those that climbed out of that pit. They were in my first thought and reactions. That could be me and what pit did I avoid or climb out of" and that could still be me down the road, maybe I could lose my job, A child, my wife, those things that we don't want to talk about but here is the key: WHAT are they going through? How did they get where they are? Does anyone ever talk to them? "They are us." They don't know how good we have it and neither do we.

Okay so where do we put these beautiful people, the homeless, do we have a spare room, do we have a building that is not occupied that can be turned into a shelter? Do you see how many houses are abandoned, buildings just closed up and not being used, while they build more? Why couldn't we start something with that? Could we start a pantry or a food bank for the hungry? A starter house for families down on their luck, trying to get a job before they move on? Some just need to talk to someone! Our comfort zone is so large we cannot find its boundaries. I know mine is, we will never be able to do enough, we can feel good about what we do but a true Believer in Jesus the Christ will never satisfy the hunger to reach out for more to help others. What we as Americans have forgotten in this Monopoly game board world of competition and pleasure, is at the feet of the Statue of Liberty It reads "Give me your tired, your poor, your huddled masses" and as Followers of Jesus Christ what this world needs now more than ever is God's Love and he already loves us all we just need to know that and that where our Love comes into the picture there's that great commandment John 15:12 My command is this: Love each other as I have loved you.

TIME OF NEED

What is your need today? Are you questioning God about something? What do you think the world can do for you, that God cannot? These may be some of the questions you might be thinking about right now. You're not alone! If you are looking to the world for answers in your time of need you will never be satisfied, they are only temporary answers. They may be the ones you want to hear but they will not be the words you need to hear.

The world is temporary, it only appears to be right on the surface, Shallow or short termed. God is Eternal, you may not see Him but he is always present.

Col. 1:15 NIV 15. The Son is the image of the invisible God, the firstborn over all creation. All through the Bible, A proven, by the world book of historical events. It says in the Great Commission. Matt. 28:19–20 NIV 19. Therefore, go and make disciples of all nations, baptizing them in the name of the Father, and of the Son, and of the Holy Spirit, 20. and teaching them to obey all that I have commanded you. And surely I am with you always, to the very end of the age."

God is eternal in his words, the answers you seek will last for all time if you allow him to live in you. If you ask the world; how do I deal with this, or what do I do now? The answers are temporary. In Psalms 118:5–6 NIV it says: 5. When hard pressed, I cried to the Lord; he brought me into a spacious place. 6. The Lord is with me; I will not be afraid. What can mere mortals do to me? 7. The Lord is with me; he is my helper. I look in triumph on my enemies.

What else do you need to give to the Lord, come to him and share your burdens just as Jesus said in Matt. 11:28 NIV 28. Come to me, all you who are weary and burdened, and I will give you rest. Come to Him/God, not the world!

TODAY'S WORLD

I had a conversation with a friend this weekend about world issues and vengeful thoughts came up.

Politics, even on the issues that are wisdom based and understandable are starting a hate in this country the likes we have never seen before. The protests that seem to be of hollow reasoning and evil that is broadcasted right out in the open and probably a satisfaction of an, "I am right you are wrong mentality," are playing a part in more ruthless conversations. You cannot have an opinion without a lawsuit.

This reminded me of a conversation with my daughter a few years back. We were talking about parents and other people and the treatment and abuse of children. She made the statement "Does God really forgive those people?" At times in my past it bothered me to the point that I had vengeful thoughts on those situations myself, but as I told my friend;

No. 1 we cannot condemn, it is not for us to do, that is Jesus's job, (John 5:30) NIV by myself I can do nothing; I judge only as I hear; and my judgment is just, for I seek not to please myself but him who sent me,"

No. 2 who are we to talk about the Sin of others, we need to examine ourselves before." (Matt. 7:5) NIV You Hypocrite first take the plank out of your own eye, and then you will see clearly to remove the speck from your brother's eye. Also "refer to No. 1"

No. 3. (Rom. 3:23) NIV For all sinned and fall short of the glory of God. A sin is a sin, there is no grading system the only unforgivable sin is denying the Holy Spirit "refer to No. 1"

We have a Savior that went the distance, a perfect Savior that is God in the flesh, Jesus the Christ that died on a cross with our sins, all of our sins. So whatever it is we have done or do in "our" sinful nature we/you need to ask for his forgiveness for and stop sinning because only he can forgive sins however we are to forgive others or he will not forgive us.

John 3:16 NIV 16. For God so loved the world that he gave his one and only Son, that whoever believes in him shall not perish but have eternal life.

WHAT'S YOUR FUEL MIX RATIO

The Holy Spirit is like oxygen to your lungs but is directed to your soul. I thought of that today in terms of how we muzzle or muffle it. I am a backyard mechanic; if I don't know how it works, I learn by all means available. Sometimes it's a sit down and study the book, and sometimes it's a trial- and-error thing. I prefer trial and error if I have a replacement part available for a spare.

I was thinking about this metaphor as the Holy Spirit was speaking. It's really something how He can put a correlation between two different subjects, I just smile and say to him "work your wonders," I'm ready when you are God! When he is silent he's still working, I get disappointed when I haven't heard from him, but ooooh if I'm patient and wait, what wonders he puts into my heart that leads to the paper his words make it into!

The thoughts of today had to do with what a carburetor does for the average engine. The best way to describe this ingenious invention is to first mention that this kind of mechanics is almost obsolete. You won't find many of them on the Automobiles of today. But the ingredients that you need to run it are the same so this concept is basically the same at least for my illustration and comparison. The comparisons, if you think about it are very similar, I will give you three: 1. Every living thing needs Air or Oxygen and Food or Fuel! 2. An automobile engine needs Air or Oxygen and they also need fuel in order to run! And the subject that I have been given is 3. Our spiritual bodies need fuel as well it's called the word or the Bible and the breath of God or the Holy Spirit.

The proof is this, If you take away either of these things it will die. If you take the Oxygen away from a living thing it will cease to exist, if you take Oxygen or Air away from an Engine it will cease to run. The same goes for our spiritual body if you ignore the Holy Spirit's prompts or direction your spiritual bodies will not be serving the Lord as He has intended. In the same way, if you put your hand over the carburetor where the air is directed it will stall and not run right, if you hold it there long enough it will stop running all together. As we all know if you put your hand over your mouth and nose you will have hard time breathing and the lack of oxygen can be fatal.

In the same way muffling or ignoring the Holy Spirit will not help you grow as a child of God. You starve out his words, his direction from our Lord and Savior and if constantly ignored you will be missing out on so much. How can I describe the feeling I get when the Holy Spirit is near and is touching our heart your soul; It sounds corny but it's like you're a Kid again and you go and get 1 scoop of ice cream and the guy running the Dairy throws in another scoop and puts a bunch of sprinkles on and hands it over and says, no charge you got the last scoop and I just had to finish it up, enjoy."

The one thing that stands between us and God, that's right "one thing" when we need or want to speak to him is the Holy Spirit. The Holy Spirit is the only interpreter between us and God through Jesus Christ. The "Trinity" it is not as confusing as some people think. We all have the same components if we are believers. God is the entity, the mind, Jesus is the Flesh that came to us and died for our sins, and the voice that speaks Gods mind is the Holy Spirit. Listen for that still small voice when God speaks, you do not want to miss it!

PART 3

GOD'S PLAN

A SONG FOR YOU

We are all a song to be heard, little pieces of our life written throughout our days and sown in like cloth. It's all a plan! The cords, the
plot has been laid, the words have been written and Gods plan is
in motion for each and every one of us. He knows all the ups and
downs. He sees it all played out, the good, the bad and again this is
why he visited us in the flesh as Jesus the Christ, to show us the way
and the path of Righteousness. We need to believe it! Speak to him
in prayer and listen to the Holy Spirit for His purpose for us. Life is
a melody for Gods purpose?

Is God asking me the same question he asked Peter before he
ascended, in his subtle ways? Finding myself in deep waters and
fighting my way to the top. Lost in a forest for hours in an unplanned
fasting and praying for a calmness to get through with no food or
water, an unplanned stay in the hospital in the middle of an epidemic
that had nothing to do with covid but kept me separated from all my
family, God was always there through it all I know that because I felt
his presence on the way to work right before I got Laid off in 2014. I
heard the words in my soul "ARE YOU READY FOR ANOTHER
CHANGE? Yes I was baffled until lunch when the doors closed and
someone was guarding the door and there was a lot of us in that
room. I teared up and smiled another proof of his plans I might as
well have heard the Lord say I AM is with you until the end of the
ages. So what are you not hearing? Ask God to open the eyes and ears
of your Soul and listen for and to the Holy Spirit he will get the mes-

sage to you. John 21:17 NIV The third time he said to him, "Simon son of John, do you love me?" Peter was hurt because Jesus asked him the third time, "Do you love me?" He said, "Lord, you know all things; you know that I love you." Jesus said, "Feed my sheep.

AN OLD PRESCRIPTION

I do not mean to upset anyone with this message in a time where Covid runs ramped, for I myself as you may know went through a 2-week stint in the hospital and it was not covid but Pneumonia and Valley fever, not knowing the outcome. It was a sort of mental anguish for myself and my family that could not visit, I relied on my Lord for everything I hoped for and as always. He provided Spiritual stability.

The Lord gave me a work of the soul today. In prayer I spoke about those who are deprived of a healing process, the people who are confined in Hospitals, Nursing homes and their own homes, they do not have the prescribed physical contact of family nearness or camaraderie that has proven to improve health and needed within the healing process.

I feel in some way that just maybe some of us if not all of us have put the Lord so far from us throughout our busy lives that like Abraham and Jacob, God wanted him to train his focus on "Him." So he put the one thing that Abraham and Sarah had wanted all their lives on the line, their son Isaac, their only son, to test where Abrahams heart really was the love he had for his son or the Love of God who gave them their son.

I wonder if this might be applying to us, not to a fateful ending but a test as to where we stand with our Lord and Savior. We need to fix our eyes more on God the father, Jesus the son who suffered more than we will ever know and the Holy Spirit who drives us to eternity through the words and prayers of forgiveness.

Question to ask over your time alone through this epidemic:

How did you handle your trial through this epidemic?

Did you speak to God More or Less in this time of confinement?

Do you feel tested and do you feel spiritually stronger in God now that it is somewhat normal again?

Read: 2 Corinthians 12:7–10 7. Or because of these surpassingly great revelations. Therefore, in order to keep me from becoming conceited, I was given a thorn in my flesh, a messenger of Satan, to torment me. 8. Three times I pleaded with the Lord to take it away from me. 9. But he said to me, "My grace is sufficient for you, for my power is made perfect in weakness." Therefore I will boast all the more gladly about my weaknesses, so that Christ's power may rest on me. 10. That is why, for Christ's sake, I delight in weaknesses, in insults, in hardships, in persecutions, in difficulties. For when I am weak, then I am strong.

ANSWERS, A LETTER FROM MY DAUGHTER

"I want to live for you, Lord. I want to serve you, and I want to give up everything that you don't want in my life. I surrender everything to you, Lord, use me for your greater plan!" This was and has been my prayer for a long time. Ever since I got back on the right path and going to church again after years of not going, I wanted to dive right in. I wanted and still want to be at every church service/Bible study/ activity that the church has. If I could live at the church I would, I hate to leave church. When my husband is with me, he wants to hurry and get going so that we can eat, but I just want to linger and fellowship and be among other Christians. I just love God and love to be around others who love God. There have been a few times in the past years that I have had to leave church due to something with the daycare kids or something just happens, and I seriously feel like crying when I leave church without hearing a sermon that is just how I am. I also love to serve, and so I have been in children's ministry at my church and my old church teaching classes with kids from 2 yrs. old–12 yrs. old.

Just the other day, we got back from a trip to Arizona to visit my family. While we were down there, I had a lot of time to think and reflect on what God's plan for our family is, and what we can do to serve Him more, it really helps that my dad is so open with his faith and relationship with Christ, he has no problem talking about God and just praying with anybody on the spot. In fact, he is one of the prayer leaders at his church which we went to the morning after we arrived in AZ. This is where my reflecting started. At the end of the service, I asked my mom where dad was, because I just felt a huge need for my dad to pray with me. She said that he was up front because he was one of the prayer leaders. I thought, "Ok, so I wanted dad to pray with me, I could either wait until we are home and we have a chance, or I could just walk up front and ask him to pray with me." So, I search for him through the many people trying to leave church and I spot him right up front. I look around to see if anyone is coming toward him to ask for prayer, because I would hate to interrupt, but there is no one headed that way. So, I head up to where he is at and I ask him to pray with me. He says, "of course" Obviously caught off guard that his daughter was coming up and asking for prayer. So, while he is praying, tears are just flowing down my face. I have so many things that I need prayer for, I have so many things that seem out of place in my life, that I don't even know what to pray. I just listen to my dad while he is praying over my life, my family, our purpose, and God's blessings on us. When he is finished, I tell him all that I can really think. "I just want to do what God wants me to do, I want to live for him, I feel like everything is chaos, and sometimes lam so confused!" My dad tells me that I am doing what God wants, and that it will be ok, and some other things I can't quite remember, but so encouraging. I knew that I was doing and serving where God wanted me, but I was so confused because I felt God wanted more of me, he wasn't done. But I, being a planner, wanted to know what God wanted, when he wanted it, and I wanted details. I wanted an instruction manual. I love to have a plan that is what is so hard with my faith sometimes, because I want to just know everything ahead of time so that I can plan. Well, that isn't how God works. He doesn't always reveal his plan to you all at once, sometimes it can take years, but it is good to know that He has a plan, He knows, and His plans for us are good! So, throughout the week that we were in Arizona, I kept thinking, looking, reflecting and just enjoying the calmness and relief of a busy, on-the-go life. I kept feeling like God wanted me to focus more on him, his children, people who need him and less on the busyness of life, other people's opinions, and just things in general that have hindered me from being what God wants me to be.

You see, for many years, I have been wanting to be what he wants me to be. I have had the desire to dress how he wants me to dress, raise kids the way he wants me to raise them, give up things that he has wanted me to give up. But the way that I looked to find the answers to these things was not what he wanted, because it took my focus off of his ultimate purpose and had me focusing on minor details that should come in second to him.

Since I wanted to please God, I also wanted to make sure I dressed right, so I looked to other people to figure out how I and my kids should dress to please God. So, my daughter and I wore skirts for a while, her mainly to church, because she hates skirts and dresses. We no longer wore bathing suits, but we didn't go absolutely nuts with it. And after some people that I looked to for role models were able to wear jeans, I figured it was ok for us to get more lenient with our dressing. This was the wrong thing to do, and this past week I realized that things like this had taken my main focus off of God and onto what other people thought. I do not blame the people I looked to for this, I blame myself. I felt this past week that this had changed me, and made me different, and I didn't like it. I asked my husband if it would be ok with him if my daughter and I could have normal bathing suits and he said it would be fine with him. So, we went shopping for some bathing suits that we felt comfortable in and are modest. This got me thinking that my focus was too much on what exactly we should wear and making sure it was right, instead of really talking to God about it. I would get so confused, because those that I was looking to be an example of what God wants us to be may have dressed the part, but in other areas went in the total opposite direction.

I felt this way this past year when my husband and I went on a double date with our friends a couple of times. The first time, they told us they wanted to watch a certain movie that was rated R. I felt really uneasy, but I figured if they are watching it, and we don't have the kids with us, we are adults, it should be ok. So, we did, and it just didn't feel right. I have felt for such a long time that God wouldn't want us to watch things like that, so we shouldn't. Then we went to another movie with them, and it turned out to be worse than the first one. In fact, I was ready to walk out of the movie theatre, I didn't realize they even allowed things like that on movie screens. It was downright dirty. And that is exactly how I felt after watching the movie.

So, I was confused. You are supposed to dress right, but you can watch stuff like this? Also, you are supposed to dress a certain way, but it is ok to get tattoos? I started questioning a lot of things including drinking. I know some Christian couples that are totally against having a drop of alcohol, I also know some that have a drink every once in a while, and sadly, I know some that drink all the time. This has left it hard for me to find exactly what my stand on it should be. (Once again, I was looking to people to form my convictions). So, for the longest time, I was against drinking at all. I figured if you are a Christian, you should not drink at all. So, I did not drink. Then after a while, I figured that it would be ok to drink some wine on my anniversary with my husband. All of these things I have been looking to people for the answer from other people. I was SO wrong!

God had brought all these things to mind last week in Arizona, and so on the last day literally right before we left, (everybody was in the van but me), I puked out all of my confusion on my dad. Meaning I just let it all out, I wanted guidance, I wanted answers. Why do I keep looking to people for guidance when it is God's plan? Who better to give the answers than the One who wrote my story? I don't know the exact words, but my dad simply said that I can look for the answers, but the one I need to go to is God, I need to pray and ask Him what is right! I knew this but I wasn't living it. I was looking for answers from this world, that only the one who holds the world has. Being in the world but not of the world has a whole new meaning to me. I need to look to God for guidance first and foremost. I need to look to Him for answers to all of the questions. If I need to, go seek counsel from the wise who are walking in Gods path and who give advice from the book of truth. God's word is truth that is where the answers are. God has given me a desire to learn so much more, but now, my head is clear now and I can focus on His plan more!!

Permission from: Crystal Noel Middleton

ARE WE BEING TOO SAFE?

So I ask you; are we being too safe? Are we feeling scared at what the world has turned into? I sit here in the middle of Gods beautiful creation in a small guard shack and wonder what will be here in five, ten, or twenty years from now!

I didn't hear Cal's Message this week, instead, I went to a different church to hear a man speak who after two years in the Navy lost over 60 pounds of flesh bones and muscle in the blink of an eye. I won't give you the whole story it is still being written by the Holy Spirit through this man. He was in Vietnam on a river gunner boat with the seals and the brown water Navy. He said on one particular day things didn't feel quite right as they were going down the river, something was wrong. He decided to pick up a Phosphorus grenade and as he prepared to throw it, a sniper was apparently attempting to shoot him in the head and instead hit the hand with the grenade.

This turned into one of the greatest sermons I have ever had the privilege of listening to. He didn't confine his message to veterans as a lot of people might think. One of the statements he made went something like this: Some of us have scars like these, but there are people that deal with scars unseen, Divorce, bad upbringing, broken families, etc. etc.

His name is Dave Roever. If you ever get the chance to hear him or go to see him speak you will not regret it. I guarantee, you will see a real walking, talking miracle that has his eyes on Jesus Christ. He had just gotten the word about churches in Egypt that had been bombed as he started to speak. We have seen what is going on in Syria with chemical attacks. China and Korea are talking about retaliating; Russia hasn't made up their minds where their loyalties lay.

Dave made a statement no one wanted to hear, "look how many countries are in this, we are looking at WWIII people," are you ready? Are you part of the body of Christ? With the hate that we are seeing, our missionaries being murdered, churches being bombed, the only question you should be thinking about right now is "are you ready for Jesus to come into your life." God has a plan for your life, it may not be what you want, it may not be comfortable but it will be for the Glory of God. There are reasons we have scars, if we don't have scars we will never know how to act or help others move on or live a life for God and be an example for him. Those without Him need to see God in us. They sang a song at the service I truly love "No longer Slaves" by Johnathan David and Melissa Heller, I like the line "I am a Child of God"

PS: This is only memory of this sermon please do not quote any of his words that I summed up in this, Buy his books on Amazon!

YFICA Russ

ARE WE CHOSEN?

The Holy Spirit put on my shoulders a past that I had not quite figured out until Sunday and I am still not sure of what to make of it. I started to remember how close to death or in harm's way that I had been at a lot of times in my Life.

I was spurred into this thinking, by a strange but innocent turn of events. I got up to go to the restroom at the tail end of the sermon and as I was headed toward the door into the vestibule a man yelled he's having a seizure; "Is there a doctor here" and a cluster of security and parishioners and I am sure I heard someone say, "I am a doctor" headed to where the person was at.

I stood there with a blank look on my face and thought what do I do, "PRAY," under my breath I did just that and that is where the Lord touched my soul.

Memories started flowing into my mind of situations, places and events that I had somehow been averted from. Accidents that happened in machinery spaces, visiting a ship whose gun mount exploded the day after, working on a ship that disaster struck days later that killed sailors in firerooms. Going on duty right before or just after a Hurricane hit, ETC. ETC. ECT.

I've said it before and ll say it again "With God there are no coincidences," I believe there is only Faith, Conviction, Hope, Love and Forgiveness but one thing I am absolutely sure of; If you listen and I mean listen with every fiber within you, we can hear our Lord through the Holy Spirit in ways we cannot repeat. That first time you recognize it, the proof will be shown to you and you will want more and more of those faith quenching miracles that you just witnessed, and do not expect small or huge just be prepared listen for that still small voice, look for that out of place situation or the lonely person on the corner. The Lord chooses you because there is no one else like you and he has you out there to speak his words into lives he will put in your path. Heads up, no advance notice, here we must always be prepared. Psalm 139:14 (NIV).

I praise you because I am fearfully and wonderfully made; your works are wonderful, I know that full well.

ASK GOD

If God can do what you don't want to do, why don't you ask him and let him work on it for you? There are examples all through the Bible, but if you don't want to read these, take a look at the miracles that are happening all over the world and every day. Go ahead google it, if that's the way you look stuff up.

In this world people have gotten so used to doing things for themselves, "even Christians", that they usually find out that it was indeed the wrong thing to do. I think we get that mentality from our parents we just don't realize that our parents ran into that same situation and got into arguments, into debt, or had painful experiences even to the point of divorce in some cases.

So what are we supposed to do? We can wallow in our self-pity and just get more and more miserable about it, doing it our way and not achieve anything but more debt, more grief and a lot of stress? Speaking of stress, if or when you have this experience, you have given doctors another paycheck and really it's for nothing. If you are you are losing weight or your stomach is tied up in knots, or you're getting headaches, or feeling listless over something you know to be wrong, the Holy Spirit has been tugging away at you to reintroduce you to Jesus Christ and you are trying desperately to ignore that voice that you know to be the right one to listen to. That is probably what is causing your illness or you're over eating problems or your weight loss. I can tell you from experience, that conviction which is what it; is not a recommended diet, it's dangerous in more ways than one.

If you went to a plumber and asked him to fix your sink because you didn't understand how to do that job or it was just too difficult, would you thank them after you paid him? Of course you would and God has given you an unlimited warranty when you receive him into your life, in essence he has paid himself for the work, when his son Jesus Christ died on the cross and rose from the tomb. So this person has gone out of his way to love you he has literally gone out on a "limb" for you.

John 3:16 16. For God so loved the world that he gave his one and only Son, that whoever believes in him shall not perish but have eternal life.

CHURCH AND STATE

We brought up the subject of Politics in the Prayer room. We get so caught up with the worst of things in this election. I for one am glad that our Minister intricately brought up what is wrong with this world today and how the pleasing of the majority, no matter how wrong our faith says it is, is being served up into the new right of the people! Either these people want to allow it, or their sin needs to be justified for the benefit of their own conscience!

Then he hit us with a sledge Hammer that a lot of us might not have been thinking about. What he was describing was Rome BC the world over 2000 years ago and it happened more than once; wham doesn't it sound familiar rang out? Everyone thought he was talking about the U.S. right now and he wasn't, but he let us put it together without even saying a word about the current problems.

We can blame certain politicians for any, and everything, we can point fingers at our current president about all the wrong things he's done to bring this country down, but what does God want us to do no matter what? "Pray for our leaders", "Turn the other cheek", "Love those that persecute us", "Love our enemy's and pray for those who persecute us." What was the greatest commandment?

Matthew 22:36–40 (NIV) 36 "Teacher, which is the greatest commandment in the Law?" 37 Jesus replied: "'Love the Lord your God with all your heart and with all your soul and with all your mind.'[a] 38 This is the first and greatest commandment. 39 And the second is like it, Love your neighbor as yourself.'[b] 40 All the Law and the Prophets hang on these two commandments."

This is when we need to speak to the Lord about any and everything concerning politics and our feelings. We need to ask him to take care of it, if we pray for vengeance, it might just turn and bite us.

We know God has a plan and it may be easy or it may be hard, but we need to except the fact that He does have "a plan, His Plan, the perfect plan I "Let's not forget we are not of this World when we accept Jesus as our Lord and Savior and it is a hard thing to do because we give in to our Human behavior and that is what the devil wants!

What are we showing those that are watching; what message are we telling those that are watching?

John 17:22 Prayer for all Believers 20. I am not asking on behalf of them alone, but also on behalf of those who will believe in Me through their message, 21. that all of them may be one, as you, Father, are in Me, and I am in You. May they also be in us, so that the world may believe that You sent Me. 22? I have given them the glory you gave Me, so that they may be one as We are one- 23. A) I in them and you in me so that they may be brought up in unity... YFICA

COFFEE FOR AN INSPIRATION

I went to get Coffee this morning at our favorite place "you know where," well are just uh all one big family down their precursor to we are all family no matter where we are! Love everyone yep that's what God says that's what we do, it just comes natural to me. Anyways "Sonny the manager" started this "pick one write one" box." Talk about a challenge I picked right up on that." What a cool idea, I turned it into a write one, pick one and pass it on, usually at work.

See on my job, I look for a smile on everyone's face and I try to put one on their face. Well today in our devotions I asked the Lord to heal me, among other things of course; "other people in our lives and things that we want to draw to Gods attention." It's not that he doesn't already know, but the Holy Spirit exercises our souls, he wants us to listen to him and use him. The Holy Spirit is that little voice you hear, the nudge in the right direction, tell you not to go to that somewhere you should not be or those things you should not do. When you're a follower of Christ that is where the definition of right from wrong affect you in a personal way. John 3:16 NIV 16. For God so loved the world that he gave his one and only Son, that whoever believes in him shall not perish but have eternal life.

This is a guideline to eternity with our Lord, after humanity messed up in the beginning there really was no way to reach it. I believe in one God that created this world and everything in it, I also believe that he came to this world in the form of flesh and blood to become one of us but pure without sin to die on a cross for the forgiveness of sins and now we have all three as one, God the father, Jesus the Son and the Holy Spirit the very breath of God and this is how he speaks to us.

Well back to this morning; when I came up to put cream in my coffee I grabbed a blank note and wrote "God heals, Just ask him" and then I picked my message out of the box and it was something that said "Have a beautiful day" with hearts on it. I was inspired by the prayer this morning and I asked the Lord to heal us. I do this almost every day, especially when I have hurt myself or worked so hard on something that I didn't think I would recover. God comes through every time sometimes not right away, sometimes it would be a couple of days but he comes through for me.

Let me ask you this, if a person or anyone were to ask God to heal them because of that note or in desperation read it as an act of faith do you think they would recognize God when that healing occurred.? You would see the power of the lord in that little note because they may just believe that there is a God!

It only takes one word sometimes or an entire speech to inspire someone, granted it could go either way depending on what it is about and what needs to be done or said; For example, One word In the heat of Battle, "Charge," -going into battle to win the fight or these Speeches, "I have a Dream "Martin Luther King's inspiring speech of creed and color as one people under God, as it should be. Or the JFK inaugural Speech "Ask Not What your Country can do for you" inspirational, so to start working for our freedom to get involved don't be part of the problem be part of the answer.

It all comes back to what the God had put in the Bible!

John 13:34–35 NIV 34. "A new command I give you: Love one another. As I have loved you, so you must love one another. 35. By this everyone will know that you are my disciples, if you love one another."

People "Take Heed in what you say to others, you or they could inspire great things for God but not without him. Just a word of encouragement could change a life or a word with the nudge from the Holy Spirit could even save a soul from ending up in hell.

DEJA VU

Ever wonder if God uses string around his fingers for reminders? That would be a lot of string!

Throughout the turmoil in this world right now do you think Gods plan is at work even though it looks grim? Have you ever noticed that the older we get the more things we give up? I used to go fishing, a lot, sometimes every day, I used to shoot archery, and I used to hunt and shoot guns a lot. I loved those things and I loved being able to do them. But you know, I have learned as I grew older that those things are not as important as what God has planned for us. I never stopped believing in God and what Jesus did for us and is doing every day in our lives, I just kept swimming upstream for the challenge not realizing that He wants to make it a journey to get there, so we know what to do the next time he calls our name. Yea we or at least I ignored him because we are bent on figuring it out for ourselves.

Recently I replaced two parts on my wife's car it took me three hours to do the one side and when I got done I went right to work on the other side and guess what? You know I learned how to do that job easier and with less pain and it only took me less than an hour. That's a learning curve of three to one.

I think this is what God expects; in fact he's seen it so many times in us I know he does? That's what "free will" does to us. It's like putting a little ten-year-old girl in a fully stocked up kitchen telling her how to bake a cake and then saying "It's all yours" and then leaving her on her own for about 2 hours. Yep and she probably doesn't even know what a measuring cup is.

The Lord deals with it, he's already got the broom and dust pan out just waiting outside the door. He already knows what the mess looks like and just like a good father that can't stand to see the tears from his little daughter or sons face, he is there to clean it up and he reaches out and holds us in his arms and he forgives us when we ask him to. He tells us everything will work out I've already seen to it, even before you were born. So when we see the world as it is today, with the protests, anger, hatred, and atrocities, pick up your bible and look up how many times this world has gone through this before. God has chosen someone that listens to him and he gives him the words to lead us out of it even to the point that others will see him in us. Like Noah you better get right with the Lord get into the boat or drown because when that door shuts there was no getting in and no getting out. Does he have a plan? God is reading the book over and over waiting to call us in and one of these days there will be some that won't be able to say "I've changed my mind." Everyone has an expiration date and only our God knows when that is, no matter what the circumstance is. YFICA

DIY

How many times have we just done things our way? If it is easier, better and the end fits the means what is the issue, right? So your boss might not have thought it out the way you did, that's a maybe, or maybe it was a test all along, to see if you could do that job exactly as you were told.

I thought of this today after reading of the plight of the Jewish people in Exodus from Egypt, Moses came a long way; from a baby on the Nile, to a prince of the Pharaoh, to a murderer of a slave driver, to the man we all know as the leader of the Jewish people out of bondage through the desert across the red sea and around in circles for forty years in the desert to the promised land. Funny when you list it like this, it sounds like a trip to grandma's house gone badly.

Getting lost walking across Death Valley only to find out your ticket to the Promised Land had been revoked, but that's the question everyone seems to be thinking of when they read these passages in Exodus. What went wrong? The last time the Jews whined about water what did the Lord tell Moses to do?

Exodus 17:4–7 NIV 4. Then Moses cried out to the Lord, "What am I to do with these people? They are almost ready to stone me." 5. The Lord answered Moses, "Go out in front of the people. Take with you some of the elders of Israel and take in your hand the staff with which you struck the Nile, and go. 6. I will stand there before you by the rock at Horeb strike the rock, and water will come out of it for the people to drink'" so Moses did this in the sight of the elders of Israel. 7. And he called the place Massah[a] and Meribah[b] because the Israelites quarreled and because they tested the Lord saying, "Is the Lord among us or not?"

Now after the Ark of the Covenant was built and the Ten Commandments were given to Moses; again, we run into the people's complaint of no water. This time was different! Numbers 20:6–12 NIV 6. Moses and Aaron went from the assembly to the entrance to the tent of meeting and fell face down, and the glory of the Lord appeared to them' 7. The Lord said to Moses, 8. "Take the staff, and you and your brother Aaron gather the assembly together' Speak to that rock before their eyes and it will pour out its water. You will bring water out of the rock for the community so they and their livestock can drink." 9. So Moses took the staff from the Lord's presence, just as he commanded him' 10. He and Aaron gathered the assembly together in front of the rock and Moses said to them, "Listen, you rebels' must we bring you water out of this rock?" 11. Then Moses raised his arm and struck the rock twice with his staff' Water gushed out, and the community and their livestock drank' 12. But the Lord said to Moses and Aaron, "Because you did not trust in me enough to honor me as holy in the sight of the Israelites, you will not bring this community into the land I give them."

All through Deuteronomy and Numbers was law and intricate details on law and punishment of every sin known at least up to this point. So I guess the answer we are trying to wrap our minds around is pretty obvious now. If Moses was given all these details, then he should not have missed the one that ended up making him lose out on what he was set out to do for all of his people.

If God is this detailed about such things and I truly believe he is, man should not be the angry one, as Moses was on that day. God is the one that wants us close to him, so much so, that he sent his only Son Jesus the Christ, who is God in the Flesh, to die on a cross and give us of his Holy Spirit for the asking. To invite us to His table when He comes again, we only need to ask forgiveness for our sins and believe that this is what happened and why.

John 3:16 NIV says it best: 16 For God so loved the world that he gave his one and only Son, that whoever believes in him shall not perish but have eternal life.

So what is holding you back? Do you understand the Love of a father that has always been there with you. The invisible GOD was once visible as Jesus Christ. When Moses asked who I shall say sent me, the answer to us will always be astounding.

Exodus 3:14 NIV 14. God said to Moses, "I AM WHO I AM. This is what you are to say to the Israelites: 'I AM has sent me to you.'"

There will never be an argument about a name or an answer like this, then or even today. No one can challenge it, and no one could doubt someone that grew up a prince of Egypt and was Jewish in acts for part of his life to come up with an answer like this on his own.

FACES

You just can't erase these faces! Sometimes it hurts when your memory of someone or something comes into focus. Sometimes it makes you happy when revisited by family or friends. When you lose a loved one, a close friend, spouse, or family member, they're faces stay in your mind until something triggers them back into your memories. I just recently lost a very dear friend.

"You know it's ironic how vivid memories become when we lose someone." You spend your latter years telling them you "don't remember" and when they're gone you just can't forget this subject came up as I was watching a John Wayne movie. I saw all his familiar stances, the old rolled front of his hat and the different faces he made that make him so alive to me. That's what actors do, they plant you into the film or story and you're so caught up in it that soon you will know every word and move that he or she makes throughout their career.

When I saw the Movie "The Passion of the Christ" it was a totally different situation. To see our Lord or the portrayal of our Lord by Jim Caviezel was to see a kind forgiving face turned into a tortured bleeding but forgiving face. This is a face I choose not to forget, while no one knows what our savior looks like physically it is clearly sketched through his works and miracles to save us with his forgiveness, No we cannot erase these faces, But the face of our sacrificed Son Of God can and will erase our sins with the blood he left at the foot of the cross.

FAILURES

I don't feel that I am in the same ballpark as most Authors. I have written Poetry at Sea when I was in the Navy and was always on the list of those that say "I'm gonna write a book someday." But when the Lord spoke to me a few times, certain human unexplainable things happened in my life for which I "without a doubt" chalk up to the Lord. I intently started not only Praying, (which I will always consider conversation through the Holy Spirit and Jesus Christ), but listening to the whispers to me and wrote uncontrollably everything I was told from the Holy Spirit. I was so enthused by what he gave me to write I knew there had to be a purpose for all this. Thanks to the Lord a publisher contacted me over questions of a book via the Lord once again shows up therefore Xlibris published "His" book "GODS POSTS". The Holy Spirit even made me look back at my past experience in Painting and said you need to Paint the story as well and so I painted the front and the back covers as well.

When you are in doubt you should read this: I recently heard the story of Thomas Edison in a video by Chuck Swindoll: When Thomas Edison was interviewed by a young reporter who boldly asked Mr. Edison if he felt like a failure and if he thought he should just give up by now. Perplexed, Edison replied, "Young man, why would I feel like a failure? And why would I ever give up? I now know definitively over 9,000 ways that an electric light bulb will not work. Success is almost in my grasp." And shortly after that, and over 10,000 attempts, Edison invented the light bulb. How will we handle our failures? It's Gods Opportune moments like these that gives us his perfect work for we are all in the body of Christ.

FREQUENCY ILLUSION

I think we have all had the coincidence of buying something popular, maybe not but for some strange reason you start to notice everyone else has got the exact same thing. No, it's not a, "Keep up with the Smiths thing." So, you buy a blue car, all of the sudden blue cars everywhere same with the exact color, or even worse the same brand, year and color. It turns out, your pick was not as special as you thought it would be. Believe it or not there's a name for it, I just looked it up yep there's a name for everything these days, it is called "Baader-Meinhof phenomenon," or "frequency illusion". I am impressed, put a check mark up for the Google bucket list. I bring this up because of the same thing that happens when we, my wife and l, do our lessons some times' The subject turns out to be the same in all the lessons or the scripture is touching the same subject or I feel something coming to mind out of the blue and then it comes to life in someone we are led to talk to, that needs that thought, or that finger to point into the right direction.

Now under an engineer, a non-believer or even in a dreamer's mind this would be called a good practice or a good idea. To think an idea or a plan of action and then follow through with it to success, that would also be neglecting to thank the Lord for those thoughts or idea's. God may give you free will but it is all part of the big plan he has for you and others that are involved. People of Faith that believe in God, those that are followers of Jesus the Christ, know, if not right away soon enough, that there is a Holy Spirit and that intercession is taking place in all things happening that others would say is coincidence. It is the only way the Born-again believer can describe it, there is no coincidence and no wisdom greater than God our maker. When you get those feelings, you know, the short spurts that come at the right time or something that makes you feel uneasy and the answer to it is right in front of your face but you don't look up or maybe you have had it happen a couple times and you don't want to look up; my dear friend, that could very well be God trying to get your attention through the one way he has, his Holy Spirit and the way that it happens is called intervention. If we decide to ignore it we are missing an opportunity to do Gods work, to help in a miracle that he has set into play through you.

Have you ever felt like someone wanted to speak to you or you needed to talk to a certain person out of the blue?

GOD'S TIMING

I love the timing of the Holy Spirit. Have you ever noticed sometimes it comes in bundles? If you are praying for help or guidance and one word that sticks out over the day's journey, or something you said to someone or should have said to someone is gnawing at you, you should be on your knees or find a quiet place to speak to God and when you talk to him, that area that you thought you forgot comes up in the "simplest" or in some cases "annoying" messages.

His time is always perfect and his words always hit close to home. The joyous part about these streams of events is the indisputable evidence that God exists not that you didn't already know but you actually see Him at work where you are or whatever your involved in and that he is not just paying attention to you all the time, but he is standing right beside you all the time. Want to do something crazy? While you are in the middle of nowhere look over your shoulder and say Thank you father for being with me today, every day, and in every way show me more. Then listen for that quiet, gentle voice that Elijah heard on Mt. Horeb.

HIS NOT MINE

I don't know if this is what I read before I commented before but again, this is so reassuring to read other than the book that I wrote and repeated in some other ways through another publisher. I feel a lot of other followers of Jesus Christ that write on Facebook have ran into self-doubt at times about the thoughts of the content, the paranoia of taking or adding to the Word of God. We pray a lot over the works that we put out. I still accredit all writings to the Holy Spirit which is of God.

Words don't just passively come to mind, there is no such thing as luck, and when a doctor cannot explain something just reversing to a healing in minutes or before a now unnecessary surgery that means God has stepped in to show that there are indeed miracles in this world and around us. So when we on Facebook write something true to heart and especially the soul after feeling, seeing or hearing so strongly that we scramble to write it down or look for that person it is meant for, It is the Holy Spirit and I feel Jesus at my side.

If ever in doubt whether the words might have come from myself instead of the Lord through His Holy Spirit, I pray about and hold onto it until I am sure through those prayers that it is for his glory, unless it is obvious to which I eventually destroy it. Those times come and go but it is in the hands of the Lord for he gave me/us this gift to write.

JUST ANOTHER STRANGE AND WONDERFUL DAY

I am not a parent that has favorites and I kid around a lot with them about that, there is no big deal with it, but I have to say that our youngest Daughter is one of the most dedicated Christian women I know, Mother comes in a close second but that's a whole different story, considering my Mother taught me about our father in Heaven and Jesus Christ in the first place.

I only bring this up because we had a week with her and Vic her husband after driving all the way down here from Ohio with six kids. Her and me speak our hearts and from our hearts.

They have three children they foster and she runs a daycare for the state out of their house. Oh, did I forget to mention she loves, no adores children she is fostering two girls and a baby boy. Anyways I, by sheer accident, have learned about a ridiculous game. You see we went to Freestone Park in Gilbert AZ. to have a nice picnic before we went home from Pikachu Peak. There were maybe 4 or 5 cars there. The weird thing started happening when I saw people walking around us aimlessly from, I don't know where and then more arrived in the parking lot. All of them starring at their cell phones. I must have counted at least 50 people that were walking around us and the surrounding area then my son in law started in and my daughter in law started doing it. I finally popped the question that was on me and my wife's mind; what in the world is everybody doing? Nobody answered so now I'm the one out of the zone finally my son Wesslee perked up and said oh it's that Pokey man thing, you look for an imaginary character on your cell phone until they appear, after you find them "I don't even want to know what they do with them then". I thought I was in a horror movie, just couldn't shake that weird feeling. Believe it or not my first thought and I repeated it out loud was it is too bad we can't get people like this to follow Jesus in the same way. There were a couple things that happened after that and I have said this before, "there are no coincidences with God."

When I went to get a sandwich, I had been reading one of Mark Battersons Books and I was on the Chapter "Guaranteed Uncertainty", "You can't plan Pentecost" with the subtitle "Are we there yet." I folded the book and walked away. Then I heard the wind coming, in Arizona we have something called "Dust devils," These are short lived whirlwinds that come out of nowhere some are quiet whisps and some can be damaging little backward tornadoes, here's the thing that is unexplainable… you can't make this up. I still have page two that didn't get away that I had wrote, and only have one copy of a paper called "From Point A to Point B". The dust devil, or God finger leafed through my book and sent all these papers into the air along with another paper I had wrote previously, I watched, and hoped that they would all come back down from at least 20 to 30 feet in the air before going over a wall bordering some houses. The only sheet that didn't come back to me, was the last sheet of three "From point A to Point B."

I think the meaning of this if you think about it is it was meant to be, I never went after it, my daughter immediately reminded me with her comment, "It must have been Gods will".

I was taken to Paul in Greece Acts 17:16–34 Speaking of A statue marked as "the unknown God."

So, tell me, was it a Coincidence? Naa, I am a Born-again Christian who prays and listens for our Gods Holy Spirit. Pokey man? No "maybe it's just another unknown God of today sorta like Paul's day in Athens, except this one you literally can't see without a cell phone. No, I believe our God wanted this particular page to go to someone in need of those words? I sure would like to see the persons face when the Lord reveals himself through that piece of paper!

JUST WHO'S PLAN IS THIS

While reading the lesson today it brought the weekends festivities into more of a perspective then I ever expected. The lesson was on; Jonah 1:1–2 NIV The word of the Lord come to Jonah son of Amittai: 2. "Go to the great city of Nineveh and preach against it, because its wickedness has come up before me. And Jonah 7:17 17. Now the Lord provided o huge fish to swallow Jonah, and Jonah was in the belly of the fish three days and three nights. And then 2:10 10. Then the LORD ordered the fish to spit Jonah out onto the beach.

The activities I speak of was a trip to San Diego with Cathy my wife where I met with new friends that were on my Ship in the Navy at a later time then myself. The closest to my era was one year after I left the old girl, "the Ship". I started thinking about the irony of the lesson and how these different years of fellow sailors were in the belly of this big fish of iron and steel. Our childhood left us there and adulthood began. While most of us felt invincible, now we look at it in a whole different light.

Some of us in that group are followers of Jesus Christ, some are not. We did things we are not proud of and we face our convictions at a later time, some then but age has a cold finger that touches us later In life, I know, I've been there, and I know that all believers will see that day at least once before our lord takes us into his arms.

So my shipmates from different times all relate as we talk old times and while we relish those days. The fish spews us out into the real world, the one he has been preparing us for since the day of our berth and before. I miss those days but I regret not living it the way God wanted me to. I am positive the people of Nineveh went through the same regrets.

I loved the Navy, I loved my Boilers, the Sea and the comradery of my fellow sailors. I leave that all behind when I love my wife even more. But God, the Father of us all, the Son, Jesus Christ our Savior, and the Gift of the Holy Spirit "the breath of God himself" I love more than anything. Fair Winds and Following Seas brothers. I leave you with this question: What perspective is God putting on your souls and minds that might be taking away from yesterday and to Him yesterday, today, or even right now? **John 3:17**

"For God did not send his Son into the world to condemn the world, but to save the world through him."

PLANNING

You know, sometimes you do all the right things to get something done. You go into it thinking, you have the patience of a snail. Then you start to wonder "where is the boundary for patience."

From start to finish, when do you finally pull up stakes and move on, or say enough is enough or throw in the towel, you wonder why aren't things working out? Why doesn't this part fit, I did exactly what the instructions said to do and it just isn't working.

In Gods eyes you could put the footer down and the corner stone on it and not be the one to finish it or enjoy what you were set out to build. In Gods eyes you may give any person a pat on the back and it could be the confidence for a lifetime or turn that one individual into the next Billie Graham in order to bring thousands to God. The Holy Spirit is the very words the very breath of God and since Jesus the Christ is not with us "in the flesh," we have become the very hands and feet of Christ, to honor God within his great commission. We can "think" our plan is a good one for our future, and it may take us far, don't get me wrong, having goals is a good thing, but the question we all, at times forget to ask is: "Whose goals are they supposed to be?" So let's put it altogether. If we rely on God when we ask him what, "his plan is" and let him share it with us, He will prosper us and give us so much more because it is his plan. He does not want you to rely on your own thinking.

Isaiah 55:8–9 (NIV) 8. "For my thoughts are not your thoughts, neither are your ways my ways, "declares the Lord. 9. "As the heavens are higher than the earth, so are my ways higher than your ways and my thoughts than your thoughts.

Proverbs 3:5,6 (NIV) 5. Trust in the Lord with all your heart and lean not on your own understanding; 6. In all your ways submit to him, and he will make your paths straight.

Job 38:34 (NIV) 34. "Can you raise your voice to the clouds and cover yourself with a flood of water? 35. Do you send the lightning bolts on their way? Do they report to you, 'Here we are'? 36. Who gives the ibis wisdom or gives the rooster understanding? (Ibis, is a large wading bird)

SCRAPS OF PAPER

Do you ever write a word, a small message, or a short sentence that you just didn't want to forget on a post it note or just any scrap of paper that's handy. I am telling you, what you may think of those messages, you may not want to ignore! When your Pastor tells you that it is good to journal, he is speaking on the ways that the Holy Spirit speaks his messages to and through us. At times I have written messages that I have long since forgot about and God through his Holy Spirit is speaking his thoughts to my soul, my heart, and my mind and I have set it aside. Later at just the right time that message will surface out of nowhere, sometimes years later and for reasons I may never understand the writing continues.

Just as this time of year comes to us in the celebration of the start of God on earth, written centuries ago, it goes on from the old to the New Testament and now that purpose has been carried out. It was spoken to the Prophet Isaiah many years before.

Isaiah 49 "Listen to me, you Islands; hear this, you distant nations; before I was born the Lord called me; from my mother's womb he has spoken my name. "This was speaking of Jesus Christ the story of our Savior Jesus Christ This was the scrap of paper all those years ago in Gods hand that was fed to the prophet's 'Isaiah 49, Jeremiah 23:1–8, Moses in Gen. 3:14–15, and Micah 5:2.

Hundreds of years later someone picked up those pieces of paper and continued writing it. It was God again but this time He is in the flesh, born to eventually bear our sins even as to death on a cross. A grim future for a mere human but for God it was the only way he could make it possible for us to be with him in Eternity.

So the story goes on even today, this is God at work through us. I could write a note with the intention of finishing it today, but God has other plans. At just the right moment God makes me or us wait until a time he has prescribed. The message is of God, for God to us, for you. This is Christmas for us, as he has proven it then; he is proving it every day and that long awaited message on a simple scrap of paper will be finished in His appropriate time for all those that will bring others to him. Those people that are hungry for the truth, they are hearing but not listening, looking but cannot see, touching but cannot feel, they will see, touch and feel those messages and that will be the appropriate time for them.

Have you ever had something come into your mind that you couldn't shake while you are in an awkward situation or it's sometimes annoying because you are in a hurry to get somewhere? Don't let it slip away, its Gods within a window of your time testing to see if you know what is more important. Ask yourself this; who is this message for? Who has God intended it to reach? "Merry Christmas to all especially those still searching".

"THIS IS A TEST, PENCILS DOWN"

A lot of people that want to deny what they feel about God, what the Holy Spirit is saying to those who are fighting the acceptance of God. It's like the conversations between the three "so called" friends of JOB. Eliphaz the Temanite, Bildad the Shuhite and Zophar the Naamathite, in Job 2:11 while he was sitting in that pile of ashes and scraping off the sores with the pottery clay off of his body and speaking to the Lord about his not wanting to be born. We all have or will hit that low moment in life when it seems like everything is against you whether you are a believer or not. The difference? If you are a believer your faith may be tested just like Job's, probably not that bad, but Job was an "absolute" in a devastating loss in order to prove a point to Satan that he would be faithful to God and JOB passed that test and was rewarded in the end and those mockers were punished. (In JOB 42) Like the sacrifices of so many men and women of God in our recent history that have overcome, they stayed the course, they didn't back down, some to the point of death.

If you are not a believer it is easy to put off sins, you simply lie to yourself, and if you haven't been paying attention to the Holy Spirit, you will continue to ignore God, the trinity, and the belief of the savior Jesus. So when the Holy Spirit does speak to you, "I pray" you will listen and act and follow that lead to Jesus the one who gave it all. If you ignore what the Holy Spirit puts on your heart and mind, you will be one of the Lost that will eventually go to Hell. They don't want to be reached and are in love with the worldly ways and worldly possessions, they think that they will take it with them, "they just can't let go," I call this being spiritually shortsighted.

These people cannot see beyond this world. The comment "When I die there is nothing else left, that's it." "You live and die and then there is nothing." They have condemned themselves indeed! We need to get these people to pay attention, they will have their moment! Whether they seize that moment, is up to them. It will be their choice of the "free will" that God gave us, will they use it wisely or be sent to Hell at the time of judgement. Matt. 10:13–15 13. If the home is deserving, let your peace rest on it; if it is not, let your peace return to you. 14. If anyone will not welcome you or listen to your words, leave that home or town and shake the dust off your feet. 15. Truly I tell you, it will be more bearable for Sodom and Gomorrah on the day of judgment than for that town.

TODAY OR TOMORROW YOUR FINAL ARRANGEMENTS

Are you ready or are you putting it off, until when? You do realize that you could die without any notice within the next second! I do not want to be the barer of bad news but are you living on borrowed time?

Do you know that when you are living for God he has a purpose for you and if he wants you to live in that purpose and you are truly loving God and believe in what he is doing and has done for us there is a better chance you will live a longer life!

If you are waiting to have life your way and think you will have the time to come to him and ask forgiveness for your sins and ask Jesus to come into your heart believing on the fact that He died on the cross for yours and my sins? You might not exist in these next few minutes, no matter how good of shape you are in! Things could change in the twinkling of an eye. Definition: In the twinkling of an eye;

[Immediately; very quickly; at once. *Just call us on this number if you have any problems, and we'll be back in the twinkling of an eye. Don't worry, boss, I'll have this report typed up in the twinkling of an eye!*]

If you watch TV I am sure you have seen those irritating commercials about a close friend dying without even a clue, He or She just dropped dead in his or her tracks and did not having any "final arrangements." This is not the absolute final arrangement I am speaking of. I speak of the next wakeup call when you open your eyes from this world into the next. If this scares you… it should. Are you prepared I don't like thinking about the fact that I could have "missed the boat" when it means eternity in Heaven or Hell.

I think of the Farmer who just kept storing grain away: Luke 12:20–23 NIV 20. "But God said to him, 'You fool! This very night your life will be demanded from you. Then who will get what you have prepared for yourself?'

21. This is how it will be with whoever stores up things for themselves but is not rich toward God."

22. Then Jesus said to his disciples: "Therefore I tell you, do not worry about your life, what you will eat; or about your body, what you will wear. 23. or life is more than food, and the body more than clothes.

This is a wake call God is watching and waiting for you to check in before you check out and times like these that policy is going to be void before you take care of those final arrangements.

UNDONE

Can anything be undone? There are no do overs! When you say or do something you regret you can't take it back. There have been more science fiction movies about this subject than I can count and while they are funny, sad or seem to be just a false Sense of reassurance, simply said "it's a "fantasy."

Everything said or done is just that, already said or already done, no back to the future, no stepping back in time, no retracting. What's done is done, what's said is said and the person on the receiving end will either let it go or it may even devastate that person's day or life.

I have a saying I put together both God and age has taught me; "One word can launch a thousand ships; one word can change a thousand lives."

James 3:3–6 3. When we put bits into the mouths of horses to make them obey us, we can turn the whole animal. 4. Or take ships as an example. Although they are so large and are driven by strong winds, they are steered by a very small rudder wherever the pilot wants to go. 5. Likewise, the tongue is a small part of the body, but it makes great boasts. Consider what a great forest is set on fire by a small spark. 6. The tongue also is a fire, a world of evil among the parts of the body. It corrupts the whole body, sets the whole course of one's life on fire, and is itself set on fire by hell.

God has an answer for that; the best thing we can do is speak to God first.

No matter what blank thoughts or fancy words you come up with, without the Lord your words are either short lived or meaningless, and a quick fix is not the answer, that just adds insult to injury. After speaking to the Lord, the best medicine is a speedy "Please forgive me" and the sooner the better. What happens after that is what I feel sanctioned by God and only if you are sincere?

WE CAN'T DO JUSTICE (TO GODS WORK)

There was a joke going around about a Scientist or evolutionist that Challenged God Himself. The Scientist stated aloud that "We don't need you anymore God". We now have the intelligence to make our own food, produce our own water, and make or fix anything that gets broken including the skills to heal anyone of anything that comes along. We can even make our own humans. We simply don't need you God, anymore. God finally spoke; humans, hmm, "you can make man?" The Scientist said "yes we can" and God said "Okay, show me "The Scientist said "You're on." Then he reached down and picked up a handful of dirt. God said "I'm gonna stop you right there, That's My Dirt" I took pictures of the sunrise today, Gods paintbrush is always stroking across the plains of his own created canvas of the world and everything else he created. His brush has always got just the right amount of whatever color needs to be throughout the world, (His canvas). Capturing this on camera can satisfy a lot of lookers, but to the one taking the pictures it's never good enough, it's not as clear, or as crisp as you see it. As you all know God created the eye, now that was perfection at its finest, we should never expect less from our maker. So when we see something ugly at least what we think is ugly or something bad at least in our definition, or the news or people bickering aimlessly on the TV- we should remember, that out of all this that we see, or get angry about, agree or disagree about; God is looking down or standing beside us trying to tell us, "It's okay I got this, I have a plan and all of this is going to work out just the way I planned it. So, when people go astray, he's there to pick up those pieces and you cannot do anything about it on your own. We just need to pray or in other words speak to Him about it and then listen for his answer. You can't do Justice like God can do Justice in all things.

WHAT PICTURES DO WE HAVE HIDDEN AWAY?

I heard a phrase on K-Love the other day about a blind man who made some statement about photographs. It was something to this effect: "My eyes are in my soul, I don't need photographs, and they are eternally embedded in my heart." I am sure that is not the correct wording but that is what I got out of it. What a concept to see with your soul, and collect them within your Heart.

That's sort of like a computer where you add pictures to a file, except you will never truly loose them. Those special ones are always there but there is more dimension to these. When you have pictures stored in your heart and you look at them, it's like a hologram the pictures are living memory, you never have to get into the attic and dig to find them, you never have to look for that shoebox, or that album. All you do is think, dream or remember your past or what your future might hold, that's even better than a computer.

Now I'm a pretty good Photographer so when I go through pictures that I don't want if they are developed pictures like from a film camera, just throw them away. However, the new thing now is Digital so now I just delete them, and the ones I do like, I correct flaws in those already taken pictures and enhance the picture before I have it Printed. What you never want to forget is when those unwanted pictures from the past start showing up, you know, the ones you were not looking for. Those memories that just keep coming back. When you have pictures in your heart and soul there is a delete button for them to, the button has a simple word on it that came with a huge price. That Button has a word and description on it that word is "Forgiven" "Jesus Christ has taken these memories from you as far as the east is from the west!"

Of course, the Lord has that "special Program" that he touches up our heart and Soul, gets rid of the shadows in our background throws out those messed up images, and blurry ones we can't really decide that we want or not but He doesn't want them either' So when we push that button or ask God for forgiveness, He's "All In" to quote Mark Battersons Book.

WHO IS DOING THE PLANNING?

Did you ever plan something out to the last nut and bolt with step-by-step procedures? Have you ever planned your day to a list of things you had to get done? Did it ever work out the way you wanted it to, or recalculate to well, "maybe if I did it this way instead of the way I had it planned" or just finish it another day? The list starts to deteriorate, the job you planned so carefully gets set back because of time or necessity.

Well, I have been planning a big job on our family car for about a month and the day is today. I have planned everything the way it is supposed to go with the book, my own knowledge and of course "you Tube."

Today's lesson was about the exact same thing, no, not fixing a car, but "preparation." Swindoll's message today was Exodus 40 Moses and the Setting up of the Tabernacle, the ark and the ritual that God gave him. A plan right down to the utensils and candlesticks, everything had to be perfect and it happened every first day of the first month. Remember Moses was chosen by God to get his people out of Pharaoh's hands, after he found out he was one of them. God got his attention through a burning bush, and at this point a lot of wondrous things were shown to those slaves that were now free. The laws then were do this or in some cases die, under the law, "yea that strict." Can you imagine what would happen today if those laws were enforced out of the blue?

"Of course, Moses did everything exactly as he was told," his instructor was the ALMIGHTY, the great "I AM" Exodus 3:14 NIV 14. God said to Moses, "I Am who I Am.[a] This is what you are to say to the Israelites: 'I Am has sent me to you.'"

I think about those two words all the time "I AM" what better description could describe "GOD." Not, I am GOD, Not, I am this or that, just say that "I AM" sent you it's an endless description.

Have we asked the Lord into our Lives, our planning or put Him into our daily activities? Imagine what would get done if we put God in front of the procedure or first in our list, not to check off but to include in every step we take. God is with us, but we need to put Him before not in the middle or after.

Surgeons have a check list and everything is laid out before the operation begins. Mechanics have their tools at the ready when needed for a tear down and a buildup and all the parts are at the ready, and Moses followed Gods plan and set everything up for his people to follow, he took his instruction from God and got the people to the Promised Land. I think we should start everything with our Lord and our Savior always.

Think about it if God can move mountains, "Matt. 17:20 NIV 20. He replied, "Because you have so little faith. Truly I tell you, if you have faith as small as a mustard seed, you can say to this mountain, 'Move from here to there,' and it will move. Nothing will be impossible for you." Luke 11:9 NIV 9. So I say to you: Ask and it will be given to you; seek and you will find; knock and the door will be opened to you.

PART 4

SALVATION AND YOUR WALK

A NEW GARDEN

During our lessons today I thought of Luke 9:23 NIV 23. Then he said to them all: "Whoever wants to be my disciple must deny themselves and take up their cross daily and follow me. I saw myself dragging around a cross, that's what it said: that if anyone should come after me, He/I should deny Himself/myself and take up our/my cross daily and follow me,"

I saw this and I also saw a long furrow following the cross, a deep one and it was almost never ending in length and then I saw my sins and wrongs and words that I shouldn't have said and a lot of shameful pasts in the wake of a putrid filthy dirt, but the further away I got I saw fields of and new growth in a clean soil chasing up to where I was.

What a beautiful thought and way He has planned for us when we do what he says when we take up that cross and leave all of our rotten Habits behind. It seems that cross will get lighter, doesn't it?

Thank you, Father-in-Heaven, for giving me this today in your son's precious name Jesus the Christ, Amen.

A SAILOR PRAYER
TO OUR LORD

If my ole sailors are listening this comical memory raised my eyebrow this morning. It also told me God was with me in those days of old nonmatter what other ways of the Navy and belief was out there. In the 70s we all seen the difference of believers, religions, and other habits in other countries we all experienced. Some mingled with ours some rejected ours. Our God has always been with me during wrong and right attitudes. Anyways I had a sort of routine in places to spend time "Meditating" yea that word means so many things back then. I would go down to the "Anchor Windless space" which would have some gym equipment. Normally after watch I would be with our maker sit in a cross knee position and meditate on home, my girl, my friends, family both home and on the ship. The Bible was a common with fear and need but not a regular read as it should have been. I sensed Gods presence in time of need always in the presence but not a constant of my heart and mind. I think the Lord stored a lot of the past up for occasions like these. Memory has its sermons, with God everything is for his Glory, the other stuff, as he put it, we ask forgiveness for all and he puts it as far from east is from the west.

Have you ever thought of that? Just how far is the East from the West? If you are Navy, you have all looked out on that horizon, you have all seen the sunsets that I have, Sunrise and sunsets fellas you know the curve we saw went from the East to the West is now more prevalent to us today than it was then. While we called it an infinity. We know that just as the great I AM, an explanation to us for GOD the map to Him is in that infinity we saw every day we walked out on deck. Your rate never mattered. I loved the crew and sailors I served with Fair Winds and Following Seas Psalms 103:12 12. As far as the east is from the west, so far hath he removed our transgressions from us? YFICA Russ

AIRWAVES, LASER BEAMS, AND WI FI

Do you know that these things exist? Do you go to your car knowing that it will start when you put the key into the ignition and turn it? Are you sure that once you put fresh batteries in your remote control that you will have the power to push a button that will give you movies on a silver screen in your living room? I've seen people blindly follow directions like a GPS on their phone to an invisible character named Pokemon in the middle of nowhere daring anyone or anything in their path to possibly harm them in that endeavor. Why is it that men, women and children can believe in a "Wi Fi" signal that you can't see, but when it comes to a God that proves himself to the world with miracle after miracle and an endless history of miraculous signs, all they can say is, "who would do that?" There are hungry people out there that feed on stories without merit. They live for any explanation about life, belief, or existence and bury themselves in scientific explanations to satisfy their questions. They have a misplaced direction in their lives and as I have learned in our Small group all of us need to work on introductions! We need to introduce them to our Lord and Savior Jesus Christ directly. Yes we cannot physically see our God but there was one time back in the day that he was flesh and blood like us and we didn't recognize him then. As he said in the upper Room amongst his disciples when he made his comeback and Thomas did not believe; John 20:28–29 NIV 28. Thomas said to him, "My Lord and my God!" 29. Then Jesus told him, "Because you have seen me, you have believed; blessed are those who have not seen and yet have believed."

ARE WE EVER TOO LOST? "HALF EMPTY OR HALF FULL" WE ARE NEVER TO LOST!

Where I work, I see a lot of people throughout the day. Some know they are supposed to be here but I'm in an area you can lose your way pretty easily, so I direct them back on the road and put them in the right direction. I am sure you might know where I'm headed with this message and I got to admit it wasn't my message but after two people came to my gate on the North end of town when they needed to be on the complete south end and on the same road I am kind of leaning on the Lord's prompting.

I think we all get lost at one time or another. We have turned left when we should have turned right, walked into the wrong room in our own home because we are just too filled with the day. How many of us have been spiritually lost at one time or another or "still are" or know someone who might be even now?

We are not getting any younger, are we? As much as we would like to say "I'm not that old yet," think this one out; how will it all end. Are you going to live a long life?

I do not want to scare anyone but the reality is, we just don't know. Old age may be the way it happens, but, Like the Bible says "you are just a vapor that appears for a little while and then vanishes away."

Yes in James 4:14–15 14. Why, you do not even know what will happen tomorrow. What is your life? You are a mist that appears for a little while and then vanishes. 15. Instead, you ought to say, "If it is the Lord's will, we will live and do this or that."

So I look at it this way, if we live for ourselves and not for Christ than we die to ourselves, but if we are a "child of God" and have accepted him in our heart and soul and ask him to forgive us, then as it reads in Romans 14:7–9 NIV 7. For none of us lives for ourselves alone, and none of us dies for ourselves alone. 8. If we live, we live for the Lord; and if we die, we die for the Lord. So, whether we live or die, we belong to the Lord. 9. For this very reason, Christ died and returned to life so that he might be the Lord of both the dead and the living.

So knowing this even now, as you might have been taught and believed before, you are never a lost cause to our Lord and Savior! He will use you for his purpose because God loves you, remember.

Psalm 103:12–14 NIV

12. So far as the east is from the west, so far has he removed our transgressions from us?

13. As a father has compassion on his children, so the Lord has compassion on those who fear him;

14. For he knows how we are formed, he remembers that we are dust.

John 3:16–17 NIV 16. For God so loved the world that he gave his one and only Son, that whoever believes in him shall not perish but have eternal life. 17. For God did not send his Son into the world to condemn the world, but to save the world through him.

God Loves you even with all the baggage that you carry just give it to him. If you are standing in the Crossroads for the first time or you are on that line again the line between sinner and the saints, as Toby Mack put it in one of his songs.

When you decide to cross that line, God the father the Son and the Holy Spirit you are hearing right now, along with the saints and angels and all followers are here with open arms God does not fail you ever, do not walk away, feel the inspiration within you, follow Jesus Christ into his wonderful light and arms and do not look back.

BELIEVE

We believe; yes "believe," the key word, key ingredient, key to life everlasting." We the followers," need to believe in him who has done it all and with every step we take in everything, everywhere we see his works. I was in a situation that taught me yet another lesson, one that could have taken my life. I understand there is a reason for everything under the sun and that is nothing compared to what living without God and the one who died for me.

In Philippians 1:23–24 he writes of the two possible outcomes: 23. "For I am hard-pressed between the two, having a desire to depart and be with Christ, which is far better. 24. Never the less to remain in the flesh is more needful for you."

Now slipping into the water in the way that I did was a choice and I feel that it was a harebrained scheme but I was thinking about others even though the possibilities were slim to none that I could help them. Never the less like it says in Philippians 1:21–22 NIV 21. For to me, to live is Christ and to die is gain. 22. If I am to go on living in the body, this will mean fruitful labor for me. Yet what shall I choose? I do not know!

So what do we do with these thoughts, they're not suicidal thoughts, it's what becomes of us before and at the time we leave this earth. We are aliens to this world when we truly believe and confess our sins to Jesus Christ who chose us, the ones that BELIEVE in what he did to wipe our slates clean even to die on that Cross. How many times have we said "yea I believe" in passing, or in a hurry you used it as a quick get away from someone who more than likely were or are honest in the knowledge that when you say it, you mean it! Where else do you go in that desperate time? You jump in with both feet, into the heart and soul of God because your grasping for forgiveness, you have finally reached rock bottom and with no way out, you have someone close to you that needs that miracle you read about or heard about, so you get down on your knees, the way you were taught a long time ago before the world entered into your atmosphere and you pray to him "God Help me!" and you Believe.

I remember a song that Plumb sang called "I Need You Now." Listen you may not think you are good enough or it's been too long since I even spoke to God, but no matter what the case is, God has been watching and waiting for you to come back to him. Nothing can separate us from the love he has for you, me or any of us, we just need to believe. Honestly where is God in all of this? Romans 8:35–39 NIV 35. Who shall separate us from the love of Christ? Shall trouble or hardship or persecution or famine or nakedness or danger or sword? 36. As it is written:

> "For your sake we face death all day long; we are considered
> as sheep to be slaughtered."

37. No, in all these things we are more than conquerors through him who loved us. 38. For I am convinced that neither death nor life, neither angels nor demons, neither the present nor the future, nor any powers, 39. Neither height nor depth, nor anything else in all creation, will be able to separate us from the love of God that is in Christ Jesus our Lord.

Just think about the woman who sought after Jesus because of her brother Lazarus dying in bed. They believed long before this happened but they were desperate to have Jesus heal him, they believed before, they believed then and afterwards they still believed John 11:23–27 NIV **23.** Jesus said to her, "Your brother will rise again."

24. Martha answered, "I know he will rise again in the resurrection at the last day."

25. Jesus said to her, "I am the resurrection and the life. The one who believes in me will live, even though they die; 26. And whoever lives by believing in me will never die. Do you believe this?"

27. Yes, Lord," she replied, "I believe that you are the Messiah, the Son of God, who is to come into the world."

I have a friend that had "fibromyalgia" for as long as I can remember and I have worked with her for over fifteen years. She is a Born-again Christian she still goes to a Catholic Church Her and another friend of mine went to that friends Church It is also a Catholic church but it is a Charismatic Church. After it was explained to her and they told her you truly have to believe in the healing power of Jesus Christ they laid hands and prayed over her. I hadn't seen her in a while and I did not think about asking, but I remember the weather used to make her pain worse so I ask her how it was affecting her that day. She told me oh "it's gone" and she continued on with what had happened at the Church. She said "All you have to do is believe in Him and I am now healed."

We only need to believe and He will Heal you, read your Bibles and pay particular attention in these versus: Matthew 18:19; Matthew 21:22; Mark 11:24; John 14:13; John 15:7; John 15:16; John 16:23–24.

I am a Prayer Warrior as a lot of you are and can be. I have heard and seen things as I pray after I pray that bring tears to my eyes. When I pray for someone, I let the Holy Spirit have all of me so that His works will be seen all for the Glory of God. I do believe in Him in all things because He saved a wretch like me anything is possible in God through Jesus all you have to do is Believe.

DAVID'S CONVICTION

In our Daily Bread this morning my wife and I read this very powerful message; In Psalms'11, David's conviction that his refuge was in God compelled him to resist suggestions to flee rather than face his foes (vv.2–3). Six simple words comprise his statement of faith: "In the Lord I take refuge" (v.1). That well-rooted conviction would guide his conduct. I like that explanation, it doesn't make you feel any better that we are all going to have or are going through convictions of all sorts, all kinds of issues, no, the things that bother you in the middle of the night. That is the Holy Spirit telling you to call on the Lord "right now" and ask him too clear your plate, take all your baggage and forgive that nagging sin that ties a knot in your stomach. We need to learn to let God lead you away from the things that cause those convictions. As this lesson says, that well-rooted conviction will guide our conduct. Amen to that.

DEAR LORD, CAPTAIN OF MY SOUL

Dear Lord, Guide me into calm waters rock me gently as we pull into your port of call. Give us lord a clean burn within the boilers of our heart and put past liberty's far and away, as far as our compasses read from the east is to the west, for they never shall meet. And when this cruise has come to its end, anchor our lives to the home that you have prepared.

May our paint and hull never rust our hull number be bright when we reach the harbor and the red deck under the water line as we know it, be the Blood of your son Jesus Christ that take our sins away for all time for He and the Captain are one, just as the breath of his order and love for the men and women aboard.

For some, and I believe in your saving Grace. Only you direct the wind of our sails in those days of old just as you turn our screws through the waters of our lives today. As our last liberty is close at hand for the Port is heaven and our stay will be eternity. Only you could create such a grand ship and only you and your son can choose such a crew at the gangway as we choose to believe in the guidance of your son Jesus Christ at the quarterdeck of our souls! As He knocks on the door of our soul "Permission to come aboard" we the quartermaster of our lives say, "Permission Granted Fair Winds and Following Seas" as we head toward the last peak of sunrise and soon to be sunset are ahead!

DEBTS PAID IN FULL

An easily answered question for those of you that are asking themselves where will we end up after we die? Where will we go? Or where will we end up. It is a like a matter of "Dept!"

Now do not take this subject lightly as in, managing your money. If you are making a decision about money, big or small, the decision should be based the same as the question we started with.

So the question is, if you have a large or small debt in money matters you have two choices! You either pay off your debt or in a worst-case scenario you end up in court and sued to pay, or worse yet you go to jail.

Matt. 18:23–25 NIV 23. "Therefore, the kingdom of heaven is like a king who wanted to settle accounts with his servants. 24. As he began the settlement, a man who owed him ten thousand bags of gold[a] was brought to him. 25. Since he was not able to pay, the master ordered that he and his wife and his children and all that he had be sold to repay the debt.

Now let's speak of another kind of debt, let's talk a little bit about our Sins and Gods roll in this arrangement. But first let me put you in an awkward position and then ask you a question: if someone told you that your debt of a dollar, ten, twenty, or even hundreds of thousand dollars is due and it needs to be paid right "NOW" or else suffer the consequences. You are stone cold broke, "and you can't even pay the dollar." The cops are there and you have no choice but to hold out your hands and wait for the cuffs to be put on your wrists. All of the sudden out of nowhere come's someone you don't even know. He comes up to you reaches in his pocket pulls out a wad of money and says to you. I'll pay this off for you if you will let me, all you have to do is say yes, that's all just yes! "What would you do?" I know what I would do, "were talking about a desperate situation here." Let's see "Jail" or "debt free" really tough decision here, huh. Ok back to the Bible story.

Matt 25:26–27 NIV 26. "At this the servant fell on his knees before him. 'Be patient with me,' he begged, 'and I will pay back everything.' 27. The servant's master took pity on him, canceled the debt and let him go.

Now back to the other kind of debt. With this debt you have two choices as well, you either pay by going to Hell or you can have this bill forgiven. As you may know Jesus the Christ took out A Spiritual bottomless note out on any and all sins for all time for all of us if we ask for forgiveness for them and believe in what he did for each and every one of us by being crucified on a Cross.

Matt 18:28–35 NIV 28. "But when that servant went out, he found one of his fellow servants who owed him a hundred silver coins. He grabbed him and began to choke him. 'Pay back what you owe me!' he demanded.

29. "His fellow servant fell to his knees and begged him, 'Be patient with me, and I will pay it back.'

30. "But he refused. Instead, he went off and had the man thrown into prison until he could pay the debt. 31. When the other servants saw what had happened, they were outraged and went and told their master everything that had happened.

32. "Then the master called the servant in. 'You wicked servant,' he said, 'I canceled all that debt of yours because you begged me to. 33. Shouldn't you have had mercy on your fellow servant just as I had on you?' 34. In anger his master handed him over to the jailers to be tortured, until he should pay back all he owed.

35. "This is how my heavenly Father will treat each of you unless you forgive your brother or sister from your heart."

DIE MAKERS

1st Definition: A "die" is a specialized tool used in manufacturing industries to cut or shape material mostly using a press. Like molds, dies are generally customized to the item they are used to create. Products made with dies range from simple paper clips to complex pieces used in advanced technology. Prov. 25:3–5 NIV 3. As the heavens are high and the earth is deep, so the hearts of kings are unsearchable. 4. Remove the dross from the silver, and a silversmith can produce a vessel; 5. Remove wicked officials from the king's presence, and his throne will be established through righteousness.

2nd Definition: To "die" (of a person, animal, or plant) stop living: "she died of cancer". [more] synonyms: pass away—pass on lose one's life expire.

Isaiah 64:8 NIV 8. Yet you, Lord, are our Father. We are the clay, you are the potter; we are all the work of your hand. Isn't it ironic that the word "die" Is spelled the same and has two different meanings? If you make something with a die it's made for one specific thing and unless you melt it down and pour it into a different mold, it's only going to be used for one purpose at least until it's worn out. Die, as in dying on the other hand is when we reach the end of our time, were worn out or it's an unnatural reason here on earth, and we return back to where we came from, dust to dust, but our souls are cast into a "Die" also and it's a choice for us to take, God gave us what he calls (free will). John 3:16 reads, and I am sure you know it, NIV For God so loved the world that he gave his one and only Son, that whoever believes in him shall not perish but have eternal life. At that split second after you say, "please forgive me for my sins and I believe that Jesus Christ died for my sins on the Cross, If you truly believe, then your soul is forever changed and goes into His hands to mold you into a new person the likes you have never known.

You will be forever changing for the one who truly loves us unconditionally. If you choose not to follow God you will be thrown into the scrap heap where fire is unending where there is no more chances of becoming anything but Dross or what they call Foundry refuse. Foundry waste. The unbelieved and its foundries are called Hell. In the words of Shakespeare in Hamlet: "To be, or not to be, that is the question. "God is asking do you love Him. He is waiting with his arms open wide.

DO YOU LIKE TO HEAR THE TRUTH?

When you were just a kid and you thought you got away with something, did you like to be told the truth? It was like you were being watched the whole time, wasn't it? You probably felt like crawling up under a rock.

Jesus said it 25 times in the gospels. You would think that it would sink in. Each and every time "it was the truth".

It might have been funny when Ruth Buzzy did the skit of the little girl in the rocking chair on a show called "laugh in" when she said "and that's the truth", but I bet it got a little annoying hearing it over and over again from Jesus to the Sadducees and the Pharisees. It was probably because it was the Truth that they did not want anyone to hear. You know, sort of like getting caught in that Lie we talked about earlier or the denial of getting caught when you were being watched.

Now if someone called you a Lier, that might have ticked you off and possibly led to a fight. That's different then telling someone I tell you the Truth and always being able to back it up or is self-evident and always with facts that could not be disputed. Oh, it eventually got some people mad because they were stuck in the old ways. It's hard to change some people into a new way of thinking.

When all the puzzle pieces came together the priests didn't want to accept the destiny that was actually taking place before their very eyes. Something in the fine print they didn't think was going to happen until the right person they sought after finally came just as it was written in those scrolls that were only read as a practice. Someone before them with their beliefs foretold of Jesus about 700 yrs. before Christ was born… in detail that was indeed the truth by the prophet Isaiah We wonder sometimes how that would play out today or at least I do Would it still happen the same way? Now it had to happen this way in order for his work to free us from sin to be done. If you read the Bible and you think about the plan to do such a thing for us it had to happen exactly like this.

Let's state just the simple facts, God had to be perfect on earth, as one of us; that's Jesus in the flesh! He had to go through everything the hardest way possible and still be of the lineage of King David which he was by way of his mother and step father. He had to be tempted beyond human standards that none would be able to withstand so he could prove that flesh and blood could withstand it in the worst circumstances and still be as human as you and me. That would show that we have the way to resist temptation through him. After he was Baptized by John "the Baptist," He separated himself from all people and human needs by going into the desert for 40 days and was tempted by those things that we do not even attempt to be without; by food, immortality, things that would define him as a leader of the world, any and everything imaginable. He was subjected to everything we are all day and every day.

Okay so the rulers of the Jews were reading things into the Bible that wasn't what God intended. For instants the Kingdom was thought to be a seat as the King of Israel and he was going to sit on a physical throne over an earthly Kingdom. All this was God's plan to the finest detail for the spiritual Kingdom not an earthly one, Ears were deaf, and eyes were blind to it actually happening so that it worked out exactly as was told all those years ago and even as Jesus described it to the apostles. It had to happen that way, their eyes were closed to the absolute truth because He couldn't let them stop it. When all of His plan took place up to the crucifixion and through to the surprise of His resurrection it had to be the ultimate Aha moment when they finally understood and now you will understand thanks to the Holy Spirit who waits on us to ask.

So tell me do you think that the people of today would want to shut somebody up because they told the truth? Would you stand up for them? If you knew the truth and the evidence and because they were in over their head would you still tell the truth.

The older I get the more I tend to say to myself and it is more Love your neighbor or enemy as yourself or as you would want to be loved. I lean toward: make a stand for what is right and don't point fingers because you were either there once or you are somewhere close now. What did He say in Matt. 7:5: You hypocrite, first take the plank out of your own eye, and then you will see clearly to remove the speck from your brother's eye.

END TIMES

No I am not talking about Jesus Christ's return, though it is connected, I am talking about something no one likes to talk about. Sure there are those things we never want to bring up or talk about, our past, things we always wanted to do but won't be able to, or maybe even a discussion on Revelations, but as difficult as those may be, no one in my book, is really fond of talking about their own ending here on earth. As much as I want to finish that last project, as much as I want to fix that car, as much as I want to clean the house and fix everything up I want to leave this earth with things showing that I did what I could for the Lord! We need to live like there's no tomorrow, for the Lord; we need to work like there's no tomorrow, for the Lord; we need to love like there's no tomorrow, for the Lord and we need to harvest like there's no tomorrow for the Lord, not just talk about it.

We will never be able do enough to pay back what Jesus Christ did for us but his death was not his "end times." It was his and our new beginnings, new Life and now it is time to break out the instruction manual that was written so that we may live again. I'm not going to regret it if I don't, "finish the bathroom," but one thing is for sure if you miss this opportunity there is no turning back you are going down and not coming back. Matthew 24:40 NIV 40. Two men will be in the field; one will be taken and the other left. No I didn't start out with the resurrection somehow it just cannot be overlooked though CAN IT?

FOCUS

Have you ever seen something and tried to show someone else where it is? Funny thing is, it could be extremely small and only an inch away from you, or it could be huge and miles away from you. Either way the outcome of "focus" is the same. When God spoke to Jonah, he couldn't get him to see the big picture with the Ninevites. He took it upon himself to make his own decision and it cost him dearly, only then did he pay attention to what God was telling him all along.

Jonah 1 NIV 1. The word of the Lord came to Jonah son of Amittai: 2. "Go to the great city of Nineveh and preach against it, because its wickedness has come up before me. 3. But Jonah ran away from the Lord and headed for Tarshish. He went down to Joppa, where he found a ship bound for that port. After paying the fare, he went aboard and sailed for Tarshish to flee from the Lord. 4. Then the Lord sent a great wind on the sea, and such a violent storm arose that the ship threatened to break up. 5. All the sailors were afraid and each cried out to his own god. And they threw the cargo into the sea to lighten the ship.

But Jonah had gone below deck, where he lay down and fell into a deep sleep.

6. The captain went to him and said, "How can you sleep? Get up and call on your god! Maybe he will take notice of us so that we will not perish."

7. Then the sailors said to each other, "Come, let us cast lots to find out who is responsible for this calamity." They cast lots and the

lot fell on Jonah. 8. So they asked him, "Tell us, who is responsible for making all this trouble for us? What kind of work do you do? Where do you come from? What is your country? From what people are you?"

9. He answered, "I am a Hebrew and I worship the Lord, the God of heaven, who made the sea and the dry land."

10. This terrified them and they asked, "What have you done?" (They knew he was running away from the Lord, because he had already told them so.)

11. The sea was getting rougher and rougher. So they asked him, "What should we do to you to make the sea calm down for us?"

12. "Pick me up and throw me into the sea," he replied, "and it will become calm. I know that it is my fault that this great storm has come upon you."

Not listening, is the same as not Focusing There was a reason for Jonah's struggle and look what came out of it. How many times do we read about or hear about an entire people of the biggest city in the World coming to God. If God hadn't intervened look what he would have missed out on.

13. Instead, the men did their best to row back to land. But they could not, for the sea grew even wilder than before. 14. Then they cried out to the Lord, "Please, Lord, do not let us die for taking this man's life. Do not hold us accountable for killing an innocent man, for you, Lord, have done as you pleased." 15. Then they took Jonah and threw him overboard, and the raging sea grew calm. 16. At this the men greatly feared the Lord, and they offered a sacrifice to the Lord and made vows to him.

Prophets are few, and the ones who want to give up, take a break, or bide their time asking God why, are missing the big picture. Sometimes it takes time, sometimes we need to pay attention. The bottom line is we all need to focus.

Jonah's Prayed: 17. Now the Lord provided a huge fish to swallow Jonah, and Jonah was in the belly of the fish three days and three nights.

2:10 10. And the Lord commanded the fish, and it vomited Jonah onto dry land.

3:1. Then the word of the Lord came to Jonah a second time: 2. "Go to the great city of Nineveh and proclaim to it the message I give you."

When someone is pointing a finger or shouts look what we do, we strain to see what someone else is seeing. That's all God wants. It will play out the way He wants it to one way or another and not the way we want it to. So, when we look, listen and seek his direction it becomes so much clearer we just need to focus a n d it doesn't hurt to be patient. We all struggle but eventually He will get it done the way He wants it!

3:6–10 6. When Jonah's warning reached the king of Nineveh, he rose from his throne, took off his royal robes, covered himself with sackcloth and sat down in the dust. 7. This is the proclamation he issued in Nineveh:

"By the decree of the king and his nobles:

Do not let people or animals, herds or flocks, taste anything; do not let them eat or drink. 8. But let people and animals be covered with sackcloth. Let everyone call urgently on God. Let them give up their evil ways and their violence. 9. Who knows? God may yet relent and with compassion turn from his fierce anger so that we will not perish."

10. When God saw what they did and how they turned from their evil ways, he relented and did not bring on them the destruction he had threatened.

Question's to ponder: How stubborn are you? How hard is it for you to admit, accept, and ask forgiveness of God or a friend?

FOR GOD SO LOVED THE WORLD

As Easter approaches, I am saddened by the possible loss of our cat stormy. I am torn in feelings of why now? With the death of our Savior to think about and the torcher he took upon himself. Today is the time to reflect on this first, not the tv, not on the projects around the house or Easter eggs in the grass. We should be looking to the cross and the sins he sacrificed himself for as well as the day of the rolled away stone and empty grave. We go from sad to happy in this season for our Savior that loves us this much. "Lord, forgive me for my torn thoughts of our cat." It is not the same, but more importantly I am reminded of a Nomad in the desert named Abraham that had no child from his wife yet you promised Him a son from Sarah when he was a hundred year's old and Sarah was Barren and after the birth and pleasure of watching him grow you Lord tested his love for you through his heart and soul by telling him to sacrifice that son as they did an animal at the alter all the way to the point of putting him to death, but you stopped him at the point of tears and the raised weapon.

Today we celebrate that saving grace from our father in Heaven who gave his only begotten son that whosoever believeth in him, should not perish, but have everlasting life. John 3;16. It is not a child, it is a cat, we love the cat, we love our families, (kid's parents, husbands and wives), but God and Jesus the Christ we love more because without God we would not have any other amongst us even a cat named Stormy.

165

FORGED BY HIS FIRE

I watch that show on TV, "Forged in Fire!" I like how the contestants are challenged against each other in a contest of something they are equally good at doing in their normal lives whether a Hobby or has something to do with their education and love of a job they have in the area that they practice it in. A short explanation: they are starting with a plain piece of steel or iron and forge cutlery of all kinds of weapons of war in the past. They put the metal into a forge then heat it up until the metal is hot enough to form into the blade they are told they have to make. The metal is then tested as they beat and form it in countless ways and refined to achieve the product in its own beauty and sharpened to the perfection that has to be tested by the Judges.

These verses come to mind: Zach. 13:8, 9a NIV 8. In all the land," declares the LORD, two-thirds will be struck down and perish; yet one third will be left in it. 9. This third I will put into the fire; I will refine them like silver and test them like gold. Heb. 4:12 NIV 12. For the word of God is alive and active. Sharper than any double-edged sword, it penetrates even to dividing soul and spirit, joints and marrow; it judges the thoughts and attitudes of the heart.

So this is what the Spirit of the Lord has said to me today: I/ We are the blade that God has made and we are being tested by the world, our edges are nicked and rolled from the acts and thoughts of a world that we no longer belong to. As believers and followers of Jesus the Christ, we are all under the great commission that was given to the original disciples of Jesus Christ and we are part of that now that we have accepted Jesus as our Lord and savior and ask forgiveness daily. "The sword," just as the tv program depicts, is tested material, as the dust we are made from we to are molded into what God intends us to be, righteous in His name, we are tested by fire refined by His Glory. We are not of this world anymore but we are to be giving the word to others so that they will also be part of the body of Christ. Matt. 28:16–20 NIV the Great Commission 16. Then the eleven disciples went to Galilee, to the mountain where Jesus had told them to go. 17. When they saw him, they worshiped him; but some doubted. 18. Then Jesus came to them and said, "All authority in heaven and on earth has been given to me. 19. Therefore go and make disciples of all nations, baptizing them in the name of the Father and of the Son and of the Holy Spirit, 20. And teaching them to obey everything I have commanded you. And surely I am with you always, to the very end of the age."

"It will cut" from the TV show Forged in Fire

Question:

Are there times when you feel you are being forged by fire or tested by the world of sin?

FROM POINT A TO POINT B

Do you remember Math? What's the distance between point "A" and Point "B"? How long does it take to drive or walk from point A to point B? Those questions didn't mean a thing to us in school, we just couldn't figure out what Point A and B were and how it had anything to do with us, could we? For those of us that think it was all you and the forces of nature that got you through life and that God had nothing to do with your making it to point B! Point A is Birth and Point B is where it all ends, or "STARTS again depending on your eventual decision for or against God!

I ask you to look back and no this isn't an episode of, "This is Your Life." Think back to as far as you can remember. Do you remember the scrapes and close calls that you made it through? When you were a child do you remember the things that your mother said to you about a sudden illness that you barely survived? Or maybe your parents were standing outside of a hospital room because you were so sick the doctors didn't even think you would make it.

Moving a little closer now to Point B, going to school getting into trouble, did your teacher leave you off the hook, did your mom say don't let it happen again. How about almost getting hit by a car but your mom or dad grabbed you by the shirt to hold you back.

Getting closer to B you're a teenager now what kind of things did you do? Did you really think no one was watching? You had this strange feeling someone else was there, but you just brushed it off and ignored it anyways.

Maybe you did a lot of crazy things and ended up hurt in some way physically or mentally or you might have thought about ending it all even at a young age... but you didn't or you didn't succeed.

You're getting closer to B, your life has come this far, any regrets yet? Any do over requests? You think you've seen it all, you think you've been through it all, you're moving closer to B, any regrets? Have you counted the things that might have been, or should have been; military, marriage, a family? Are you thinking you didn't get enough excitement and feeling like you should've waited to settle down?

B is getting closer, it's not stretching itself out and you're making it tougher every time you think you can handle it all by yourself. Gods watching, his Holy Spirit has been tapping you on the shoulder for years. He's been whispering but that freewill thing just keeps on tugging you in the wrong direction. It feels good to make your own decisions. Do you think you know all you need to, to get to point B?

Well, the one thing you do know by all standards is that when we were not far from point A we felt invincible, almost immortal. Now the Lord is still knocking on the door of your soul, are you going to get off that couch of stubborn negativity and worldliness? Will you ask him in?

Bones creak and eyes are heavy your movements are slow. Many have went before you and many have spoken to ears that just now are listening. Another knock has come to your door that you used to see at a distance. You cannot send this one away you have now arrived at Point "B"!

Luke 12:19–21 NIV 19. And I will say to my soul, "You have plenty of grain laid up for many years. Take life easy, eat, drink and be merry.'" 20. "But God said to him, 'You fool! This very night your life will be demanded from you; then who will get what you have prepared for yourself?' 21. This is how it will be with whoever stores up things for themselves but is not rich toward God".

This all sounds like the story of scrooge and it may very well be yours. Things coulda, woulda been better, livelier and had more purpose if you first answered the knock at that door.

Only now that you realize what God has been saying all along do you have a chance.

John 3:14–17 NIV 14. Just as Moses lifted up the snake in the wilderness, so the Son of Man must be lifted up, 15. that everyone who believes may have eternal life in him." 16. For God so loved the world that He gave His one and only Son, that whoever believes in Him should not perish but have eternal life in him. 17. For God did not send His Son into the world to condemn the world, but to save the world through him.

HOME IS WHERE YOUR "SOUL IS"

As I sit here at home reading our lessons for the day I listed to the word of a Christian band "BLDG429," Where I Belong".

The words "I'm not home yet," hit me deeply as I feel lost thinking about schedules, doctors' appointments and what's next on my walk-through life, another day not yet planned out, what do we need to do today where do I have to go etc. etc. etc.

All our steps have already been meticulously laid out not by us but by our God for he is always there.

Psalm 139:8–12 NIV

8. If I go up to the heavens, you are there; if I make my bed in the depths, you are there.

9. If I rise on the wings of the dawn, if I settle on the far side of the sea,

10. Even there your hand will guide me, your right hand will hold me fast.

11. If I say, "Surely the darkness will hide me and the light become night around me,"

12. Even the darkness will not be dark to you; the night will shine like the day, for darkness is as light to you.

We need to just follow His will as we walk through our lives and Worship Him and Him alone, our worldly thoughts are nothing unless we profess just How Great our Father in Heaven is and tell Him the love you have for him and nothing else. We are striving to the place we call home, a home not made by man.

HOW IN THE WORLD DO I FIND MY WAY BACK TO YOU LORD?

In the world none of us will ever find our way back? The bible says forget your past and strive for what is ahead.

Philippians 3:13–14 NIV 14. Brothers and sisters, I do not consider myself yet to have taken hold of it. But one thing I do: Forgetting what is behind and straining toward what is ahead, I press on toward the goal to win the prize for which God has called me heavenward in Christ Jesus.

And he also said to think on these things.

Philippians 4:8 NIV 8. Finally, brothers and sisters, whatever is true, whatever is noble, whatever is right, whatever is pure, whatever is lovely, whatever is admirable-if anything is excellent or praiseworthy think about such things.

When we go through trials of the past, we need not feed them we must put them behind us they only serve the Lord with a common bond to another person, I believe, to bring them to the Lord, not to dwell on the childish things that drove you to sin, but to answer the question of: How God drove you away from them now. This is the Holy Spirit saying to you when you say I need you now Lord! I need you right now, this past is giving me knots in my stomach draw me nearer to you just as David said.

Psalms 28:1. To you, LORD, I call; you are my Rock, do not turn a deaf ear to me. For if you remain silent, I will be like those who go down to the pit.

Psalms 35:1–4 NIV 1. Contend, Lord, with those who contend with me; Fight against those who fight against me. 2. Pick up the shield and armor; arise and come to my aid.

3. Brandish spear and javelin against those who pursue me. Say to me I am your salvation.

4. May those who seek my life be disgraced and put to shame; may those who plot my ruin be turned back in dismay.

So, when we feel down and stepped on or our thought go to the extreme left or you do the things you want to do but know that you shouldn't think on this tidbit that is larger than life to us all, as sinners. Read this scripture:

2 Corinthians 12:7–10 NIV

7. Or because of these surpassingly great revelations. Therefore, in order to keep me from becoming conceited, I was given a thorn in my flesh, a messenger of Satan, to torment me. 8. Three times I pleaded with the Lord to take it away from me. 9. But he said to me, "My grace is sufficient for you, for my power is made perfect in weakness." Therefore I will boast all the more gladly about my weaknesses, so that Christ's power may rest on me. 10. That is why, for Christ's sake, I delight in weaknesses, in insults, in hardships, in persecutions, in difficulties. For when I am weak, then I am strong.

John 17:14–16 NIV I have given them your word and the world has hated them, for they are not of the world any more than I am of the world. 15. My prayer is not that you take them out of the world but that you protect them from the evil one. They are not of the world, even as I am not of it.

So how in the world do you find your way back? Step away from this world and ask God into your heart if you haven't already and let him take you to places you have never seen through His eyes and speak the words He gives you and listen to the Helper, (the Holy Spirit), through Jesus Christ from God. That is how you get back to the Lord. Read John 3:16 again! Once you accept Jesus Christ as your savior and ask forgiveness for all your sins, (those sins He died for), you are no longer of this world but the Kingdom of God.

I DON'T GET NO

I thought of a song today an old rock and roll song today. I got to thinking why do young and older people turn away from Jesus the Christ or God or church services.

I realize that we all want something, a nice car, big house, beautiful wife, you know, everything. You want to do it all now, vacations, less work more play!

From the time we are baby's, to well into our golden years, from rattles to cars, milk to wine, love for a mother and father to a wife and family. When and where does it all end?

We all know when, not the exact time but when you're dead it's all over. You no longer want and no longer care and It doesn't matter at that point.

The dash on your headstone is where you are at right now as you read this. It is that time before you are laid to rest that matters and if you are trying to do it all, there is that endless, "I am still not satisfied" feeling that you will always have.

But there is always hope! Hope in the lord. When your soul is satisfied everything else will follow, your only hunger will be more of what is always available and it works like this; more of God and less of me less of you.

Psalm 54:4 NIV Surely God is my help; the Lord is the one who sustains me.

Questions: What is it you really want in this life?

What do you think you will wish you had done when you are whispering those last words?

What Love will be with you now and forever and even after you're gone from this world?

Do you know why Jesus died for you and the words He said with his dying breaths?

Read Luke 23:26–49 one phrase stands out to all of us: 34. Jesus said "Father forgive them, for they do not know what they are doing."

John 3:16 For God so loved the world that he gave his one and only Son, that whoever believes in him shall not perish but have eternal life.

I WOKE UP ON CHRISTMAS MORN

Merry Christ mas everyone. Over two thousand years ago a baby was born in a manger, a Savior is born to us. The shepherds were told this in Luke 2:8–11 NIV 8. And there were shepherds living out in the fields nearby, keeping watch over their flocks at night. 9. An angel of the Lord appeared to them, and the glory of the Lord shone around them, and they were terrified.

{It was a fraction of the light compared to the light of the world that had just been born and it was on the turf of farm country. The good shepherd had been born) and it wasn't an announcement on paper. It wasn't a hospital contacting people to see a newborn and the crowd was not a lot of relatives (relatively speaking), it was the lowest of the low, shepherds out with the sheep.}

10. But the angel said to them, "Do not be afraid. I bring you good news that will cause great joy for all the people. 11. Today in the town of David a Savior has been born to you; he is the Messiah, the Lord.

John 10:11 "11. I am the good shepherd. The good shepherd lays down his life for the sheep.

He will also be our Savior. John 1:29 29. The next day he saw Jesus coming toward him, and said, "Look, the Lamb of God, who takes away the sin of the world! (all our sin if we only believe and ask Jesus the Christ forgiveness for our sins.)

John 3:16 16. For God so loved the world that he gave his one and only Son, that whoever believes in him shall not perish but have eternal life.

There was another Christmas Miracle not as important as our Saviors birth but it was still a miracle from our early history.

In 1914 Dec. 24th at 2pm during WW1 a Christmas Truce took place: on a crisp, clear morning 100 years ago, thousands of British, Belgian and French soldiers put down their rifles, stepped out of their trenches and spent Christmas mingling with their German enemies along the Western front. In the hundred years since, the event has been seen as a kind of miracle, a rare moment of peace just a few months into a war that would eventually claim over '15 million lives. But what actually happened on Christmas Eve and Christmas Day of 1914. The next morning, in some places, German soldiers emerged from their trenches, calling out "Merry Christmas" in English. Allied soldiers came out warily to greet them. In others, Germans held up signs reading "You no shoot, we no shoot." Over the course of the day, troops exchanged gifts of cigarettes, food, buttons and hats. The Christmas truce also allowed both sides to finally bury their dead comrades, whose bodies had lain for weeks on "no man's land," (the ground between opposing trenches.)

So what's your Christmas story, when did you see the light of the world?

We have or will see one in our life time? Don't try to explain it away when it happens, think of that babe in a manger, think about all those sins he came to take away because he loves us all so much, that he wants us to believe in him and be with him when our journey on earth is over, just as the song says in" Weary Traveler" by Jorden St. Cyr "Someday soon were gonna make it home" Merry Christmas to you all.

INTIMACY WITH GOD

What if there is a more intimate purpose between God and us than we think. I never thought of the Love of our Lord to be as strong as I have lately.

Yes, I am reading yet another book, Frank Viola said this in his book "From Eternity to Here." "Your Bible is essentially a love story." "In fact, it's the greatest love story of all time." I and that Author are speaking of spiritual love, the strongest love ever known.

I love Paul's words here but I center my attention on verse 5, this is what I speak of here:

Romans 5:1–5 (NIV) 1. Therefore, since we have been justified through faith, we have peace with God through our Lord Jesus Christ, 2. Through whom we have gained access by faith into this grace in which we now stand. And we boast in the hope of the glory of God. 3. Not only so, but we also glory in our sufferings, because we know that suffering produces perseverance.

4. Perseverance, character; and character, hope. 5. And hope does not put us to shame, because God's love has been poured out into our hearts through the Holy Spirit, who has been given to us.

Its food for the Soul.

IT IS NEVER TOO LATE

Have you ever noticed that in a split second and maybe sometimes a lot longer we think we have to handle a problem on our own? As Christians or as I have adopted from Author Carl Medearis, "followers of Jesus," we have learned from the words of the Lord to give all of our problems, burdens, pains and sins to him.

In Matt. 11:29–30 NIV 29. Take my yoke upon you and learn from me; for I am gentle and humble in heart, and you will find rest for your souls. 30. For My yoke is easy and my burden is light.

I was praying for someone online today and the words just spilled out like a glass of water and something I hadn't thought of for years was there in the inspiration of the words given. It is never too late for the Lord to answer prayer, it is literal, and I mean it cuts to the bone! This is the prayer, I don't like to repeat a prayer to anyone because it seems personal for them, but this was online and I think it will help others in there prayer life and understanding of how our Lord works in our conversations with him.

Dear Lord we know that you know everything and you know this situation right now. Time means nothing to you. So if we, the people of this earth, get the news late you apply any prayer at the exact time it is intended for, even though by our human time zones the act has already been completed.

I dear Lord believe, with all my heart and soul that you keep time on your own watch, you are capable of all and everything possible and impossible by our thoughts, actions, deeds and words!

You are the great "I am" and those words spoken by you centuries ago are as endless today as they were then. So given the fact that we are believers in you our God and your fulfilled plan for the redemption of our sins throughout this world through your son Jesus Christ's death on the cross and Resurrection from the dead. I ask you as the great and only Healer of everyone and/or everything that lives and breathes to ensure that this will turn out perfectly, In your son's precious name Jesus Christ I pray Amen.

He told Moses in Exodus 4:11 NIV 11. The LORD said to him, "Who gave human beings their mouths? Who makes them deaf or mute? Who gives them sight or makes them blind? Is it not l, the Lord? He also gave him his Name he didn't say God or Jehovah, no, he said two simple words that mean more than all the words that describe him, "I AM has sent me to you."

IN COMMON

What does a "lost lamb," a "lost coin," and a "lost son," have in common? Well Jesus spoke about all three of them, these were called Parables. These stories simplified truths in our lives, sometimes they were our truths that touch our lives and sometimes they convict us as they are intended. Oh you can dispute them all you want but these reminders were given so that you and I can relate to them. His all-time famous quote was and is, "I TELL YOU THE TRUTH." He lived a sinless life so we could see that we should strive to follow His example, Because He was one of us but He was a perfect man without flaw like Adam was before sin entered the world except, he was also God in the flesh, part of the trinity.

Jesus spoke Parables to help us understand what is happening and why, what has to change in our lives so that we will be with him one day when he returns and what will happen if we do not accept those changes before it's too late. That would be the end of our earthly lives.

So, in Matthew 18:12–14 He speaks of a man who had a hundred sheep and one wandered off. He was so worried about that one lamb that he left the ninety-nine to look for that one lamb. Now before we go on, think about someone in your family that you would literally leave everyone behind just to find that one person, mind you, they are all important but you are worried about the one that is lost.

Ok let us move to the "Lost coin." Now in Luke 15:8–10 Jesus spoke to the people about a woman with ten silver coins and she loses one! She sweeps the house from front to back and finally she spots it and oh how happy she is to find that one coin. Now I won't ask you if you had a coin your fond of, oh no. But I will ask you how happy you were when at one particular time you found the car keys that you kept somewhere for safe keeping and you forgot where, yea you probably said something like "duh," But wasn't it a relief?

The last one, is the Lost Son In Luke 15:11–32 We read a story that I feel hits close to home with a lot of people although I have to say I keep thinking it's the older Son maybe because I went astray when I left My home as a young man and I am the older Brother, but never the less Jesus spoke of a young man the youngest of two brothers who had to leave tired of chores and wanted to enjoy the world. He asked his father for what in that time was a savings for an inheritance before his father died so he could squander it on earthly things partying, gambling and women. Like a lot of stories, we have all heard about in our day and age, there is always a black sheep in the family.

He finally hit bottom lost all the money in his endeavors and couldn't hold or even find a job it just so happened there was a severe famine in the land and he was to the point of starvation. He then started thinking in panic mode what can I do to stay alive? He didn't have enough to eat on he was living with the pigs that he was tending to for a farmer but wait his father was a well-off farmer and even the workers ate well.

He headed for home and on the journey he rehearsed what he would say, (Have you ever rehearsed what you were going to say before telling someone something? Never comes out that way when your face to face does it), he was ready to hear the lessons his father would teach him, He was ready for the lecture he would get from him and he was to the point it didn't matter he would work for his father or do anything he asked he admits he has sinned against heaven and against his father, I can just see him coming over the hill toward the farm and lo and behold as he gets closer possibly tears running down his face knowing full well what has been done is a shame, he will live for the rest of his life.

The tide turns completely around as his father is running toward him with a big smile probably tearing up. For his son has come back to him alive. The son says the words that he cannot hold back any longer, Father I have sinned against heaven and against you. I am no longer worthy to be called your son. But we read that the father did not say anything to him but threw his arms around him and kissed him and then he got his servants to set up for a huge banquet and with the fatted calve to boot. Then and only then he says we celebrate for this son of mine was dead and is alive again; He was lost but now is found.

Yea that's the long one but this gives those out there so much hope because the Lord forgives and loves us unconditionally.

So back to the question at hand, "what does a "lost lamb," a "lost coin," and a "lost son," have in common? Well, all three were lost of course but Jesus was speaking of our paths and how we will all have moments when we are lost, sometimes after we have been born again to him, we will lose our way or we are still lost and haven't seen His truth yet. That opportunity will come and then you will have to make a choice but we are the Lamb, we are the coin, and we are the lost son that left home and haven't found our way back yet. We haven't suffered enough to admit there is only one way, Or have we?

The one other thing that is mentioned in these three parables that brings a tear to my eye every time is this the lost sheep: I tell you that in the same way there is more rejoicing in heaven over one sinner who repents then over ninety-nine righteous persons who do not need to repent. The Lost Coin: I tell you there is much rejoicing in the presence of the angels of God over one sinner who repents. The Lost Son: We celebrate for this son of mine was dead and is alive again; He was lost but now is found. We should all be rejoicing and celebrating when someone comes to the Lord and we really need to lift those up that have lost their way and have come back and asked forgiveness as well. YFICA

Questions:

Can you relate to these Parables?

Do you feel lost and without God?

Have you lost something like keys or a special memory written that you do not remember where you put it? If so how did you feel when it was finally revealed to you?

Philippians 4:6–7 NIV 6. Do not be anxious about anything, but in every situation, by prayer and petition, with thanksgiving, present your requests to God. 7. And the peace of God, which transcends all understanding, will guard your hearts and your minds in Christ Jesus.

Pray even for those lost things in your lives especially the lost souls and those who feel they are lost again always.

LOST AND FOUND

Why do we pain ourselves over the little things? Have you ever noticed that when we lose, or "misplace" something like car keys, a book, cell phone or your wallet, how frustrated or panicked we get looking for them? I reminded my son about how his mother and I would do just that. We finally came to the conclusion that it doesn't do us any good to fret over things when God can see where everything is at any time. Gee that would mean he has a "higher perception than we do," he does you know.

Luke 15:8–10 NIV 8. "Or suppose a woman, has ten silver coins and loses one. Doesn't she light a lamp, sweep the house, and search carefully until she finds *it*? 9. And when she finds it, she calls her friends and neighbors together and says, 'Rejoice with me; I have found my lost coin!' 10. In the same way, I tell you, there is rejoicing in the presence of the angels of God over one sinner who repents."

Even a second set of eyes might help, but still God can see all things, so why not ask him and let it go. I trust our God will tell us, show us or walk us to where it is and to whatever it is. The more we sweat it the sillier we feel when we find out that it was right under our nose all along. Now I am not saying it'll happen right away but I believe its within his time frame, and I believe he has a reason for that Journey.

That's just like our Journey of Faith. Some make it a Quest or an argument on the why should I or the, what do I get out of it. We just need to answer that knock on the door of our heart, Give Jesus all the baggage, worries and those things we lost. Jesus knows where you are but he searches for your soul and heart. His love is unconditional.

Matt. 18:12–14 12. "What do you think? If a man owns a hundred sheep, and one of them wanders away, will he not leave the ninety-nine on the hills and go to look for the one that wandered off? 13. And if he finds it, truly I tell you, he is happier about that one sheep than about the ninety-nine that did not wander off. 14. In the same way your Father in heaven is not willing that any of these little ones should perish.

By the way I found my license and my keys. And my Bible that I misplaced!!! ha ha

MAKE UP YOUR MIND

Ask your (self) do you want to be the best that you can be? Is it worth striving for? Do you think that you already are? If you do that might mean you are full of yourself.

Think about this for a moment! What sacrifice do we make every day, week, year for the one that we expect to answer our prayers at any time.

Do you know Jesus? Really know him?

When was the last time you spoke to him? Have you ever lifted anyone that you didn't know up in prayer?

We read our lessons this morning, the scripture was Joshua 24:14 and 15. Joshua was, in so many words, telling the Israelites to make up their minds, and it was their choice, and he told them the right thing to do. To throw away the other Gods and to wholeheartedly follow the one and true God that freed them. In other word's get off the fence and make a decision, make up your mind!

I took from this as putting the conviction on the people in a subtle way but giving them the decision. Then he made the stand of his Family by saying "but as for me and my family we are going to serve the Lord." I think I seen a repeat of a familiar reading of Billy Graham that I hear a lot growing up and is Toby Macs song "City on Our Knees" 15. "But if serving the Lord seems undesirable to you, then choose for yourselves this day whom you will serve."

The question still stands today just as it did all those hundreds of years ago, even as Jesus Christ in the flesh told us when he was here as our resurrecting promise was so near.

God, I love you so much and I don't deserve your promise, but I have taken it up and its mine! It can be yours, do not let it walk past you, take it up and let go of self and live with us, for Him.

I think it's time the luke warm or drifted Christian and especially those that haven't taken that important step come to the Lord. It's time we stand up, get off the fence, put self away from us and reach for the one who will save us from our sin, is reaching out with open arms, knows us intimately and loves us unconditionally.

MUSIC, IS GOD IN HARMONY WITH HIS CREATION

When it comes to our Lord, He can get your attention in any form because he is in everything and everyone and is everywhere some accept him and some do not. He is either at the door of your SOUL knocking or he is already in side making you into a man or woman of God, (to be more like Jesus), yesterday I heard the sound of Maracas by my parked Motorcycle that was under a Palo Verdi tree.

Now I had seen a build up of the seed pods dried out all around my bike for a few days. It is like the Lord picked a time in the day to make me smile, Can you think of a time something trivial made you smile or laugh and wonder what God was trying to tell you? Samuel was a young boy when Jesus called him into service for him read this:

1 Samuel 3: **1.** The boy Samuel ministered before the Lord under Eli. In those days the word of the Lord was rare; there were not many visions. 2. One night Eli, whose eyes were becoming so weak that he could barely see, was lying down in his usual place. 3. The lamp of God had not yet gone out, and Samuel was lying down in the house of the Lord, where the ark of God was. 4. Then the Lord called Samuel. Samuel answered, "Here I am." 5. And he ran to Eli and said, "Here I am; you called me." But Eli said, "I did not call; go back and lie down." So he went and lay down.

Samuel was a young boy that studied under Eli who knew his time was near and was looking for a successor waiting for God to show Him who would take his place. Then God after a long time saw Samuel and Spoke to him and then Gods plan went on.

Do we not hear the lord speak? Do we ignore him after a number of times he talks to us? Knowing God, Jesus and the Holy Spirit are one, do we decide to question our maker?

Something we call a dust devil spiraled around my bike and swirled the pods over the paved parking lot all the way across a lot about half the size of a football field. It sounded just like the Maracas that my Grandma used to shake showing us how they made noise Yes it made me smile. I watched my God sweep the parking lot with His broom and clean up around my bike. Thank you God for days like this, it reminds me always that you are in control always.

2 Sam. 6:14 14. NIV 14. Wearing a linen ephod, David was dancing before the Lord with all his might.

When the Lord talks to us that is not only a revival it is cause to celebrate. I don't like to dance but you can bet I'll be dancing in whatever way that I can.

NO LONGER A PERSONAL PRAYER TIME

I felt this today as I read the request of prayer for church and Members, our government, those out there that do not know God or at least how we know him, (as our personal Savior Jesus Christ). While most of us pray over our family, friends and meals, there are those that Pray upon request for others in need like for marriage, illness, leaders, weather, and anything that has a toll on the Human Heart and soul, like this virus we have all endured and seen the devastation in one way or another.

I cannot help thinking about a Minister from Africa that talked about his people under oppression of the leader there. He was amazed at how many showed up in Washington for the Day of prayer, "that the minister invited him to, and how well it went, but when he asked, what time tomorrow, he was disappointed to find out that we only celebrated one day of prayer this time of the year. He went on to tell us that they, (the people where he is from), have to pray fervently during the day, just to get enough food for the day and just to survive throughout the day.

Prayer is a conversation with God made possible through the blood of our Savior Jesus Christ and the work done by his sacrifice on the cross for our sins. The intercessor or translator as I like to think of him, is the Holy Spirit. So, when we have the thought of someone or something we want to pray about, the Holy Spirit will be with you within that prayer; big or small, eloquent or in a studder, partial or impartial and give it to God the way our heart and soul and mind really intended it. You never have to worry about a fancy or long-winded prayer.

If you truly want or need God to handle it for you, the Holy Spirit gets the message across. Likewise, the Spirit also helps in our weaknesses. "For we do not know what we should pray for as we ought, but the Spirit Himself makes intercession for us with groaning's which cannot be uttered." (Romans 8:26)

So if you feel as I do at times, that you want to be with that person or in that place to pray face to face because sometimes it seems it is the only way, think about what time and space mean to God! You are praying for his glory not ours. If you truly believe, then it doesn't matter, just as long as you pray.

Remember the story of the Centurion in Luke 7:1–10 Jesus healed the servant without even going to the house. He said to his followers these words "I tell you, not even in Israel have I found such faith."

John 14:26 But the Helper, the Holy Spirit, whom the Father will send in my name, he will teach you all things and bring to your remembrance all that I have said to you. Some of us pray one way or another, sitting down, standing up, prostrated face down on the ground, all day, all week or ten minutes a day. Whatever is real to you, but especially what is real to him.

Daniel prayed every day at his window and later when he was in a pit with the Lions in a den that God closed the mouth of. We are all Prayer Warriors when we talk to God and that talk is a two-way street, we need to Listen even more so. He is waiting for you to speak to him and he is waiting for you to hear Him!

ONLY 6 FEET AWAY

There is a new perimeter out today and though the devil wants to make it so with the Lord as well. Do not ignore; our God is less than 6 feet away. Though we are not to touch, hold close, hug or kiss; our God is less than six feet away. An epidemic it may be. The illness, the panic, the death we've been told, is best at six feet away We know not when our death will be, but we know our God is less than six feet away Our president called for a day of prayer and Billy Jr. did agree, what we need is to be closer than six feet away So do we follow the rule of the world at length from 0 to six feet away, Yes, that is what we must do here But our God the father, our Jesus the son and the Holy Ghost are not of this world and are the creators of it. The hunger pangs roll within those souls of the lost that long for direction in these days of peril Our Lord has sent us out to the Harvest and they are reaching The great I AM has no limits for those he loves, which are all But our short sighted minds have blinded the preaching And to fight the evil one now is certainly not a time to stall Can we really put a measurement on what or where God can go when he speaks of where he sends our sins as far as the East is from the West The Love of God will not be separated by Death nor life, angels nor demons will not part. So in the words spoken to me by him, the Body of Christ, we be, there is no measure that God to the follower be, not even 6 feet and that now you see the Holy Spirit speaks.

PRAYER

Each day of our lives should begin with prayer. Every breath we take should be a word of praise and thanksgiving for everything we see, smell, touch and taste. Where we walk he is there, when we greet others, we should speak what he breathes into and through us. We must know that we are not, nor ever will be, perfect. This is only a fraction of the ways God wants us to communicate with him.

We live in a world of distraction. We think with our own minds and not the mind and Heart of Jesus. The distractions get louder and brighter everyday, but if we breathe, walk, listen and speak from Christ who is the Light and the truth everyday, the Holy Spirit will deafen our minds and hearts to all distractions of this world and the light of our Lord and Savior will show us His light that makes even the darkness of this world even brighter than the sun.

This is Prayer! It is not a "should be" praying, it is our first priority to God that we must pray, they are our marching orders, our request for a battle plan.

You wouldn't go to war with an empty rifle would you? READ EPH. 6:10–17. He lives in and with us when we talk to him every minute and every hour of every day. "TALKING TO GOD = PRAYER"

SCIENCE FICTION IN ITS EARLIEST STATE OF FICTION

How could we view the crucifixion differently? I know some of us have thought about it, I know I have. Instead of," what would Jesus Do?" what would we Do? "What could we do?"

So if we could go back to watch and were allowed to change something in those last few days of Jesus Christ before, up to and including his Crucifixion, what could it possibly be. (Remember "you already know what it's about," you already know the outcome, but most importantly "You know the why he had to do it."

You cannot think up any scenario that would accomplish the task that Jesus Christ thought up and executed to himself for our Sins. Oh you can call it messing with the space time continuum or any other scientific mumbo jumbo but the fact remains long before scientists got a hold on their ideas. If it were possible, no changes could be made without the will of God, and his plan is perfection!

Any scenario would not work because of the lives it affected in just the right way before, during or after. Jesus was saving lives all through his life up to, during and even today all because of his final act of Love as a man of flesh and blood.

It's interesting to think about, but when you come to the "why" you hit a dead end. To witness our sins being taken away at that moment, to live through that time or die for the sake of Christ in that time would be an honor in itself. But knowing, seeing and reliving history would be gut wrenching. Watching the movie "The Passion" is bad enough, who could hold back tears watching the silver screen. But to witness in real life and not be able to move an inch out of place, even God wouldn't permit that! But it is an interesting thought for discussion.

THE BOTTOM LINE

That's what people seem to want to hear most of the time. Just give me the facts, the short version, the bottom line, that one word description. Seems this world has condensed everything. I guess it might have started with your parents saying these famous words that you didn't really want to hear, but it always came down to "Don't beat around the bush, just spit it out!" You don't need to look those words up or know the definition, that sentence speaks for itself.

When you listen to a sermon do you walk out of church knowing the meaning of that whole sermon as if you savored it to thought for a later date or take notes so you might study it later, or did your "mind," not your heart or soul grasp just one word that touched a nerve or something in the fiber of the day. Did you feel like the Preacher was just talking about you? Something offended you or made you feel guilty? It only takes one word to start a war or ask for peace, to launch a thousand ships or lead solders to victory or death. We can help that smile on everyone we meet's face or we can bring a hate upon us that will last for generations. We can tell the truth or lie; and just as it says about our tongues in the Bible James 3:3–12,

Well the bottom-line as to what our very being or purpose of our existence on this earth can be summed up in one commandment.

Matt. 22:36–38 NIV "The Greatest Commandment... 36. Teacher, which is the greatest commandment in the Law?"

37. Jesus replied: "'Love the Lord your God with all your heart and with all your soul and with all your mind.' 38 This is the first and greatest commandment.

The problem that is upon us is; At the time of physical hunger, we go to the first thing that comes to our minds "The Fridge" it's nearby When we hunger worship, we hear or see or touch things that please us, we settle for what makes us feel good. Culture wants to do what is here, close by, Material things. We are setting our souls up for what the mind sees because it is nearby. Our creator is unseen because he is spiritual; He created us for one purpose, to worship him and only him, to live for him to eventually be with him forever. In the Old Testament we have this commandment: Exodus 34:14 NIV 14. Do not worship any other god, for the Lord, whose name is Jealous, is a jealous God.

In the New Testament we have this: Matthew 4:10 NIV 10. Jesus said to him, "Away from me, Satan! For it is written: 'Worship the Lord your God, and serve him only. In John 4:21–26 NIV Jesus said, 21. "Woman," Jesus replied, "believe me, a time is coming when you will worship the Father neither on this mountain nor in Jerusalem. 22. You Samaritans worship what you do not know; we worship what we do know, for salvation is from the Jews. 23. Yet a time is coming and has now come when the true worshipers will worship the Father in the Spirit and in truth, for they are the kind of worshipers the Father seeks. 24. God is spirit, and his worshipers must worship in the Spirit and in truth."

25. The woman said, "I know that Messiah" (called Christ) "is coming. When he comes, he will explain everything to us."

26. Then Jesus declared, "I, the one speaking to you—I am he."

I read this in Tozer's book "The Purpose of Man" Jesus taught essentially that we are portable sanctuaries, and if we are worshiping in spirit and truth, we can take our sanctuary around with us. Jesus said, "Don't you see that if God is Spirit, worship is spiritual, and anything spiritual has no location in time?" You do not get up in the morning, look at your calendar and say this is the time to worship. You do not get up, go out, look around and say this is the place to worship. You worship God now, anywhere, any place, any time, because worship is spiritual.... So what is the bottom Line? People worship anything these days, they create it and sometimes without even realizing it. Our purpose is to worship and worship is spiritual, there is only one spiritual God and he made us for that purpose, "So that makes this the BOTTOM LINE >>>>37. Jesus replied: "'Love the Lord your God with all your heart and with all your soul and with all your mind.' 38. This is the first and greatest commandment.

THE QUESTION WE SHOULD ASK

During these scary and struggling times the question is not "where is God in all of this" but rather "where are we in our Faith with God in all of this?"

What are we doing in our homes that we are all more confined to? Are we looking in other places for answers? Has politics consumed us or the news taken over almost all aspects of our lives?

Has prayer turned into a hobby on the side or just for meals and bedtime?

Matt. 6:25–27 NIV 25. "Therefore I tell you, do not worry about your life, what you will eat or drink; or about your body, what you will wear. Is not life more than food, and the body more than clothes? 26. Look at the birds of the air; they do not sow or reap or store away in barns, and yet your heavenly Father feeds them. Are you not much more valuable than they? 27. Can any one of you by worrying add a single hour to your life[a]?

Look to our God for answers, speak to him, depend on him. Let him open your eyes and ears to the Truth Jesus prophesied when he was here on earth, better yet we all need to live as Jesus lived walk in his shoes and to do that read and consume what that best seller the Bible says.

Phil. 4:6 NIV 6. Do not be anxious about anything, but in every situation, by prayer and petition, with thanksgiving, present your requests to God.

THE RAPTURE

I wonder what intellect they will have on the news explaining the rapture and the disappearance of so many people. I won't be here for it but it's just a thought.

While the devil is preparing people for the Anti-Christ, God is preparing people for the Rapture. I don't know when the rapture will take place but I do believe it could be soon. I also believe this is a time that God is giving us a chance to repent.

We need to get the Gospel message out!!! Until the Good Lord calls me away from this world to go home I want to make it clear that I believe in Jesus Christ as the True Lord and Savior. Despite the fact that I am human, and I fail a lot, I believe that Jesus is the Son of God. I believe that He died on the cross as a sacrifice for our sins and that He rose from the dead on the third day. He loves us all dearly (far more than we deserve) and forgives our sins when we repent. His Word says in John 3:16 NIV 16. For God so loved the world that he gave his one and only Son, that whoever believes in him shall not perish but have eternal life.

The bible also says Matthew 10:33 NIV 33. "But whoever disowns me before others, I will disown before my Father in heaven.

This is the best challenge I have seen; so, if the Holy Spirit moves you and you're not ashamed, repeat it and pass it on.

Can I get an Amen for being a believer in The Father, The Son, and The Holy Spirit? When is the last time you were ashamed of someone you know?

THE STRENGTHS OF A CHILD'S PRAYER

The Lord gave me his thoughts of prayer and for some reason he reminded me of this Matthew 19:13–14 NIV 13. Then people brought little children to Jesus for him to place his hands on them and pray for them. But the disciples rebuked them. 14. Jesus said, "Let the little children come to me, and do not hinder them, for the kingdom of heaven belongs to such as these."

So, God tells us' unless we become as little children, we will not inherit the Kingdom. This is the goal is becoming more like Christ and following his instruction. But our conduit or "communication," to our father in heaven is prayer through the Holy Spirit and Jesus Christ. That is the plan he had for us long ago and even today, nothing too small, nothing too big.

As adults sometimes we get caught up in the world's view of speaking and listening to God. We sometimes put our own idea of what and how prayer should be when all we really need is his instruction, which is in the Bible. In those words we even have a blueprint that can be used, but this is just a model.

Matthew 6:9–13 9. "This, then, is how you should pray: "Our Father in heaven, hallowed be your name, 10. Your kingdom come, your will be done, on earth as it is in heaven. 11. Give us today our daily bread.

12. And forgive us our debts, as we also have forgiven our debtors. 13. And lead us not into temptation, but deliver us from the evil one."

The Holy Spirit concedes for us, we do not need to come up with the words; he will fill in the blanks or give you the prayer that your heart and soul wants to give to God.

I now think, in the light of this scripture, that approaching God on his level would be best done as a little child. Who more qualified than the pure innocents of a child? Can we, or do we sometimes revert back to our innocent childlike thoughts with the Lord as we get older? Remember we are all children if God or he wouldn't have said so!

THIS LITTLE LIGHT OF MINE, I'M GONNA LET IT SHINE

I want to hear that; I want to hear it again. This world, or as it says in Romans, "all creation," is going through pains as a woman goes through childbirth.

Romans 8:22 NIV 22. We know that the whole creation has been groaning as in the pains of childbirth right up to the present time.

It is waiting for the end for God to send his son for one last time. To defeat the evil that was born into what used to be a beautiful creation of Gods. Sin was made present by the first couple turning into temptation and hatred was been brought here by one brother against another that led to murder and it hasn't stopped growing since.

When I turn on the news, which I am growing quite weary of, I see name calling, anger at its finest hour and stories or ancient history being spread of things done that cannot be undone.

It is things in our past that should be given to the Lord and left there. I am speaking of "any past," take what you learn and what makes you stronger and use it for Gods purpose and there is always a purpose for God! Phil. 3:13 NIV 13. Brothers and sisters, I do not consider myself yet to have taken hold of it. But one thing I do: Forgetting what is behind and straining toward what is ahead, Luke 9:62 NIV 62. Jesus replied, "No one who puts a hand to the plow and looks back is fit for service in the kingdom of God." We have reached a point once again where if Jesus were here today it would be another reading of the scrolls as he did in Luke 4:21when he read Isaiah 61 that ended with these words; 21. He began by saying to them, "Today this scripture is fulfilled in your hearing." However, this time would be the last time and we will not get a warning like that again. 1 Cor. 15:51–53 NIV 51. Listen, I tell you a mystery: We will not all sleep, but we will all be changed—52. In a flash, in the twinkling of an eye, at the last trumpet. For the trumpet will sound, the dead will be raised imperishable, and we will be changed. 53. For the perishable must clothe itself with the imperishable, and the mortal with immortality. Matt. 24:6–8 NIV 6. You will hear of wars and rumors of wars, but see to it that you are not alarmed. Such things must happen, but the end is still to come. 7. Nation will rise against nation, and kingdom against kingdom. There will be famines and earthquakes in various places. 8. All these are the beginning of birth pains. "Quite Familiar wouldn't you say!"

THOSE MOMENTS

I think when we really pay attention to our God through the Holy Spirit when he speaks to our very soul, we enter into His light. I don't mean literally a bright light like Moses saw on Mount Sinai; oh it might feel like it because of the wisdom and Inspiration he gives us at that moment. It will be an, "all of the sudden moment", or the "Aha moment", or the answered prayer moment. It's a rush when and to those people that don't know him there really is a God and the ones who lost their way and realize God has not forgotten us! That's when Jesus introduces himself to them or to us and he takes our hand at just the right moment, that perfect timing. That's when he is knocking on the door of our heart and Soul. That's the kind of light I am talking about here, but there will be another brighter light one day.

We will walk into and follow this light to fulfill his work through the trials of this life if we follow his plan and His word some day we will all walk into His glorious perfect light and never leave his side again we will be in his arms forever no more tears, no more pain and all the love we will ever want or need.

His Promise and sacrifice for us has never left us and is open to all who come to Him.

John 3:16 NIV 16. For God so loved the world that he gave his one and only Son, that whoever believes in him shall not perish but have eternal life.

Revelations 12:4 NIV

"'He will wipe every tear from their eyes. There will be no more death' or mourning or crying or pain, for the old order of things has passed away."

God bless and keep you.

TRANSITION

Within the last oooooh, twenty-five years or so I have heard the statement from three different points in my life "THAT WAS THEN and THIS IS NOW'" Now we all change with age and trial and error, but the Lord wants us to change in a different way, every way and more every day. With every worldly subject that is brought into the foreground of our lives, it is becoming more evident to me that the Holy Spirit, "acting on the purpose and love of God," is causing a transition of our souls from the human standpoint, to the "Gain" into Gods Glory and purpose in preparation of walking with him at the end of this life of the flesh. Who are we to sort out the grain from the weeds? Who are we to benefit from these earthly laws? Let the lawyers do their job Who we voted for in an election is not of Gods realm, and the issues are not for us to decide on physically, but we can use the issues as a list of prayer concerns for what is right in the eyes of God and what HE will decide to do with them. This is our stand; we do not protest or point fingers! This is what we, "the followers of Jesus the Christ," "the Prayer Warriors," do, and in those descriptions above all others. For ours is the loving of our enemies and the aliens of which we all were at one time. This is truly our calling for and in Christ. I will simply list the scriptures that brought this message from the Holy Spirit to me. I will not write them out this time but I advise you to read and include them in this reading and see what He puts on your heart and Soul as well!

They are: Isaiah 61:1–6 and John 16:20–22.

WE ALL GET HUNGRY

I read a little part "from Eternity to Here," and felt the tug. I read and felt our God speaking as he does in unexplainable ways through the Holy Spirit. The reminding scripture is Ezekiel 3:3 NIV 3. Then he said to me, "Son of man, eat this scroll I am giving you and fill your stomach with it." So I ate it, and it tasted as sweet as honey in my mouth. I remembered seeing something similar to this somewhere else in the Bible, but it was in the New Testament.

John 6:53–55 NIV 53. Jesus said to them, "Very truly I tell you, unless you eat the flesh of the Son of Man and drink his blood, you have no life in you. 54. Whoever eats my flesh and drinks my blood has eternal life, and I will raise them up at the last day. 55. For my flesh is real food and my blood is real drink. The one thing that hit me between these two was no. 1 Ezekiel was a Prophet; God spoke to Prophets so they could speak to us and this was when God wanted to give a nourishment of the word to one that the people would listen to as a known Prophet. God wanted Ezekiel to know his words so well that there would be no dispute.

He described the eating or consuming of the words written on scrolls, why? Because, we can describe what we ate for dinner easier and at length more than we can describe words we read. Have you ever noticed that a kid or an Adult will describe a piece of pie or cake they ate? They will literally tell you what the ingredients taste like and you will remember it every time you see what looks like and how good or bad it tasted at the time.

I think the Lord wants us to hunger for the words so much that we want to describe how they make us feel. Google has nothing on that. Do you remember the hunger to find in the truth, in the word, or an "aha moment?" What word, what single word do you remember, turned your head when your mother or father spoke? What stopped you in your tracks even for the curiosity of what they wanted to say to you? I remember the word "LISTEN" and that word pretty much made me stop and listen every time through life. So, No. 2. When Jesus said when you eat the flesh and drink the blood of the son of man, I am pretty sure everyone in that group along with the Disciples that followed him were hanging on for the next words he said. I think he was describing the sacrifice for all mankind to take the sins of the world upon him. "Are you prepared for what I am about to do," I think was what he was trying to say to them and to us.

Now, what do we do with this? Well if you are not a believer as a "follower of Jesus Christ," as a courier would say "you have been served "literally god has served his son up for us so that you and I can have eternal Life after we leave this world! If you are already a believer it's time to get hungry again, it's time to taste what is in the Bible again.

Whether or not you are a believer, try this little test once if you think reading the Bible once is all you need. Read one passage, one scripture, write it down, get the meaning of it in your mind, give it a week and read it again. This is why the Bible is known as the "Living Word," The story is never over it is the TRUTH Amen.

WHAT IDOL'S DO WE HAVE?

Acts 17:21–29 21 (All the Athenians and the foreigners who lived there spent their time doing nothing but talking about and listening to the latest ideas.)

22. Paul then stood up in the meeting of the Areopagus and said: "People of Athens! I see that in every way you are very religious. 23. For as I walked around and looked carefully at your objects of worship, I even found an altar with this inscription: to an unknown god. So you are ignorant of the very thing you worship—and this is what I am going to proclaim to you.

24. "The God who made the world and everything in it is the Lord of heaven and earth and does not live in temples built by human hands. 25. And he is not served by human hands, as if he needed anything. Rather, he himself gives everyone life and breath and everything else. 26. From one man he made all the nations, that they should inhabit the whole earth; and he marked out their appointed times in history and the boundaries of their lands. 27. God did this so that they would seek him and perhaps reach out for him and find him, though he is not far from any one of us. 28. For in him we live and move and have our being.' As some of your own poets have said, 'We are his offspring.'

29. "Therefore since we are God's offspring, we should not think that the divine being is like gold or silver or stone—an image made by human design and skill.

Paul pointed out how ridiculous it was to have a statue without a name to worship. Then he used it as an example He said: My God made you and me from one man, they made a statue in their image and Paul said, "God made you in his image, God used clay and breathed life into it; you use gold, silver and stone, that's blasphemy."

One of our Sins against God and is one of the Ten Commandments in the book of Exodus 20:3–5 NIV 3. "You shall have no other gods before[a] me.

4. "You shall not make for yourself an image in the form of anything in heaven above or on the earth beneath or in the waters below. 5. You shall not bow down to them or worship them; for I, the Lord your God, am a jealous God, punishing the children for the sin of the parents to the third and fourth generation of those who hate me,

Granted this is the Old Testament but we still do not want to break a Commandment! My question to you as well as myself Is, how many unknown or known idols do we possess? Do we let them get in the way of our true and only God? You know, it could be anything in our daily living from your constant use of a cell phone to a hobby you can't seem to put down, to binging on whatever! What is it that would prevent you from going to church or introducing Jesus to a homeless person, or anyone? Maybe it's time to throw some of that stuff out or stop those time-consuming things that take our eyes off of God!

WHAT IS THE DIFFERENCE, I JUST DON'T SEE IT

Genesis 1:27– NIV 27. So God created mankind in his own image, in the image of God he created them; male and female he created them. "That was Adam," (we don't even know what the word color is at that time).

Much, much later "the answer" to the sin that Adam and Eve had created in the Garden became flesh and dwelled among us, His name is Jesus He came and lived among us and he knew no color whether we were to point it out or not, whether they were either Black, white or any other color this world offered; through his eyes or as we also refer to" God on earth," it was of no consequence then or now!

Then Jesus told his disciple's they have a job!

Matt. 28:16–20 NIV 16. Then the eleven disciples went to Galilee, to the mountain where Jesus had told them to go. 17. When they saw him, they worshiped him; but some doubted. 18. Then Jesus came to them and said, "All authority in heaven and on earth has been given to me. 19. Therefore go and make disciples of all nations, baptizing them in the name of the Father and of the Son and of the Holy Spirit, 20. And teaching them to obey everything I have commanded you. And surely I am with you always, to the very end of the age."

John 13:15 15. I have set you an example so that you should do as I have done for you.

So what Jesus wants us to do, is live by "His" example. I am weak but prefer it this way even knowing that I will never be totally as He is. But to strive is to gain, as Paul would say "run the race to win."

By doing so we must be, as I believe, as close to what Jesus is. He does not look at outward appearances; He, "in ordinary human terms, would be considered color blind." We are also not to be judgmental as he pointed out, in such a way as to set our souls in judgement of our minds, by pointing out that we are all sinners.

When he taught us about the women caught in adultery in JOHN 8:1–11, they knew the truth and their plan to trip up Jesus within the law, which turned on them.

Now we have a Holy Spirit that catches us in any sin and works in us, up to confession and conviction that brings us to our knees, asking forgiveness.

When we love the Lord our God with all our heart, soul and mind as the great commandment say's we will be guided by the Holy Spirit to act in accordance for God at all times in that fact we will be under attack and now, more than ever, we must be prepared and always read our instruction manual, The Bible, for his Truth to come alive within us.

WHEN WE SPEAK SALVATION

It's not Hieroglyphics! When speaking to others about your Faith, do not over think it, as a matter of fact don't think it. Ask the Lord to speak through you and then the words will move freely through you to whoever they are intended for.

You know your own testimony but the Holy Spirit knows how to represent it because He was the one from God that first introduced you to Jesus Christ.

In Matthew 3. NIV We find John the Baptist described through the book of Isaiah just as Jesus was for told of his coming to take away our Sins around 700 years before;

3: 1. 3. In those days John the Baptist came, preaching in the wilderness of Judea **2** and saying, "Repent, for the kingdom of heaven has come near." **3** This is he who was spoken of through the prophet Isaiah:

> "A voice of one calling in the wilderness.
> 'Prepare the way for the Lord,
> make straight paths for him.'"

So when you are describing your own testimony to others, be prepared. Ask God, who knows better than the one that he brought it to through His Holy Spirit to explain what happened at that "aha" moment when you finally came to your spiritual senses. Paul wrote to the Corinthians this

1 Corinthians 15:1–4 1. Now, brothers and sisters, I want to remind you of the gospel I preached to you, which you received and on which you have taken your stand. 2. By this gospel you are saved, if you hold firmly to the word, I preached to you. Otherwise, you have believed in vain. 3. For what I received I passed on to you as of first importance: that Christ died for our sins according to the Scriptures, 4. that he was buried, that he was raised on the third day according to the Scriptures,

"Now that is a testimony!!"

HOW CLOSE TO OUR LORD ARE YOU?

This came to mind when I prayed this morning before we read all our lessons. Before I tell you the outcome let me ask you a simple question that I think you might have all asked yourselves before. Have any of you ever known someone mentally so well that you knew what that person was going to say next or vice versa or they knew your next move? Or you knew there's? A little creepy huh, but sort of cool especially if your good friends or a spouse.

The reason I brought that up is when you pray about something or someone you are giving that concern or blessing to God through Jesus Christ with the help of the Holy Spirit. When I or we are so in tuned with the Lord in this way, which is the way that prayer works in mine, and I read my lessons sometimes they correlate with those prayers in practically the same way. I feel God is saying to me personally "I got this, thank you for giving me these concerns and blessings!"

Romans 8:26 NIV 26 In the same way, the Spirit helps us in our weakness. We do not know what we ought to pray for, but the Spirit himself intercedes for us through wordless groans.

Matt. 6:7–8 NIV 7. And when you pray, do not keep on babbling like pagans, for they think they will be heard because of their many words. 8. Do not be like them, for your Father knows what you need before you ask Him.

PART 5

GOD'S WILL

A HOLE OR A HALF A HOLE

I remember someone asking me "if you dig a hole, and then you fill it half full, what do you have? It's sorta like, are you a pessimist or an optimist, do you see the glass half full or half empty. We'll almost.

Have you ever known anyone who has a void to fill? I mean an inner void, no matter what they have, buy or want, they are never really satisfied. That next new thing they really want is nothing but a repeat of an ongoing habit, but it continues. They keep on seeing that hole half full, or the glass half empty and never half full.

Jesus talked to a Samaritan woman at a well about a similar situation. John 4:7–14 NIV 7. When a Samaritan woman came to draw water, Jesus said to her, "Will you give me a drink?" 8. (His disciples had gone into the town to buy food.)

9. The Samaritan woman said to him, "You are a Jew and I am a Samaritan woman. How can you ask me for a drink?" (For Jews do not associate with Samaritans.)

10. Jesus answered her, "If you knew the gift of God and who it is that asks you for a drink, you would have asked him and he would have given you living water."

11. "Sir," the woman said, "you have nothing to draw with and the well is deep. Where can you get this living water? 12. Are you greater than our father Jacob, who gave us the well and drank from it himself, as did also his sons and his livestock?"

13. Jesus answered, "Everyone who drinks this water will be thirsty again, 14. But whoever drinks the water I give them will never

thirst. Indeed, the water I give them will become in them a spring of water welling up to eternal life.

There is only one God that can fill that void whatever it may be. Whatever you are searching for, are hungry for, that need or want is not something you need or want, it is the unseen God that cannot be seen with the naked eye. God became flesh so that we would see Him as Jesus Christ. He lived among us and shown us His love that was rejected but his plan worked out perfectly to the point of death on a cross so that hopefully we will believe in Him as the living God that loves us and died for our sins so that we freely admit and ask forgiveness for them and will live an eternal life with Him in heaven when Jesus returns.

Picture that glass full and don't even dig that hole you will never be able to fill it, ask the Lord for that living water and you will never thirst or hunger in this way again. Satisfied yet? Pray/talk to him and see what happens he will wipe the tears of every eye!

A LIVING ACTIVE BIBLE STUDY

Ever feel guilty or bad about yourself? Are you with or without God? Have you just left him behind because you don't feel you are good enough for him? Ok, what sin depresses you, what sin bothers you the most? Mentally and physically, it hurts. We are all sinners, every one of us. We all have or do carry that burden around from our past or even today right this moment. Somewhere in your youth you have been taught right from wrong and that is where it starts. That is why you feel the way you do right now. So, let's go to the Bible, what can the Bible possibly have that would help me feel better? Well first it has examples of the things you might be going through or worse. Some of the stories are going to point to your situation, hit you hard, don't stop reading, keep going, look up specifics and it will lead you into the Old Testament which may seem pretty ugly and you may start feeling worse, make you cringe about the outcome back then. This is when you pray to God to help you through. So, hang in there, the light is truly "at the end of the tunnel." After you read this go to Isaiah 53 where God speaks through Isaiah about the savior that is coming years before he came into being. Then read through Mathew, Mark, Luke and John about the Life of that one that was spoken about in Isaiah years ago. Jesus Christ the Savior and what his eternal gift for us, for you and me for all time as he died on a cross, as the prophet had witnessed and wrote. Then go to John 3:16 NIV for God so loved the world that he gave his one and only Son, that whoever believes in him shall not perish but have eternal life. 2 Corinthians 5:17 **17** Therefore, if anyone is in Christ, the new creation has come: The old has gone, the new is here! Now get on your knees and pray thank the Lord for loving you unconditionally enough to go that far to take away your sins for all time. Pastor Greg Laurie said this in today's lesson: Wherever you are, He knows what you are going through!

A SHOULD A, COULD A, WOULD A, ATTITUDE

You know I've dealt with soldiers and sailors that have a should a, could a, would a, attitude including myself.

Yes, it is self-pity. Sometimes after they've been out for a while, they don't feel they accomplished enough for the war's effort or it ended before I could have done anything, or the one I hear a lot of since I retired is yea I wish I had stayed in longer.

Jeremiah 29:11 NIV 11. For I know the plans I have for you," declares the Lord, "plans to prosper you and not to harm you, plans to give you hope and a future.

I am no stranger to this, we all have a past that we wish was different. I was in a place in the service where I was literally not seen and at that time none of that mattered. We have this evil demon that tells us were not good enough, that there were things and jobs more exciting than where we ended up. All kinds of things that work on our minds. It's the same way with our so called, meaningless, jobs everywhere, you might be perfectly happy with your job then one day someone puts that negative seed out there and there you have it, your miserable. Why not this or why not that. Romans 12:4–5 NIV 4. For just as each of us has one body with many members, and these members do not all have the same function, 5. So in Christ we, though many, form one body, and each member belongs to all the others.

Its time though that you face facts cars can't run without gas, a battery, wheels or gears and where you are in the military, or in life is exactly where you were meant and are needed to be at that particular time. We are all important for whatever length of time we were there. So, when we have to move on or do something else it's for a cause that's greater than us and it's where we belong and our God is making those choices because that is where our work for Him takes us. 1, Cor. 12:12 NIV 12. Just as a body, though one, has many parts, but all its many parts form one body, so it is with Christ.

ARE WE EXPENDABLE?

I always thought, if you did what you were told, worked hard, got qualified in everything available, kept your nose clean and treated everyone fairly you would never be let go or fired. Well, that sort of worked out in the Navy for me, but out here it's a whole different ballgame. When a corporation or a company is not doing well it falls on everything and everyone that is not needed or is using too much of what is needed to survive, so if you fall into that category and your job isn't needed then you become "expendable. "That's when it makes sense to let that person go; at least from a business standpoint. A good analogy would be a, "sinking ship or a hot air balloon," you have to get rid of the extra weight so you either stop sinking or you are going down slower giving you more time to figure out how to patch that hole in the bottom of the boat or the balloon. I can now say I have seen this at both ends after being let go after a fierce fight with problems I thought I was fixing on my Job and then being let go. I have seen the floor pulled out from beneath me and I have seen the roof fall as well," neither were a pretty sight." Just recently I have had the unusual and sad experience of seeing someone I worked with and for, that I admired very much, let go just the other day. Reality once again has given me a wakeup call and once again age rears another truth! That it never slows down. As an officer of the VFW I performed funeral services for many Veterans that were both near and dear to me. I chose to leave that part of my life because I was tired of the heartache it created, and just as friends move away or we choose to go elsewhere, memories never escape us. But we can't give up and let it get us down, the Lord has his plan for us, we either stay in our rut, or we listen for those words from the Holy Spirit and do what he asks, when he asks. Sooner or later we will all end up looking up at him, from a Hospital bed, a battlefield, at sea or yes even possibly that Job you are working on today. At this point regret should be the last thing on your mind. So, what message do you want to leave to everyone when you go on that final journey? It doesn't really matter what we accomplish on this earth unless it honors our Lord and Savior. The Legacy of our one True God is all that matters. We need to make it known that he is always with us no matter where we go and we need to turn to him for answers, problems, that don't seem to go away and the pain and sorrows that really hurt. We can choose to run away from them or we simply ask Jesus to help us through it and watch what he does with them. The message I see here is the same as when I got let go from my job, "Never burn your bridges," always trust in the Lord and listen for the Holy Spirit to speak. If you listen for that small voice and act on it, just watch what he does next, the outcome will be Glorious "None of us are expendable to God," Not one! But with free will He has given us the choice to follow him. Don't make the wrong choice!

IS GOD IN THE PICTURE WITH YOU?

Photography is all about the gathering of light in "front" of the camera; not behind it! Isn't that what our Faith is all about, the gathering of light, for Him?

A camera gathers light from what a subject has to offer and makes a beautiful Picture of what we have seen or what we just looked at. It turns a three-dimensional image into a single dimensional piece of paper to decorate and remind us of what is out there or what a beautiful sight it once was.

When we go through life's trials or changes, good or bad, God wants those pictures. He wants that image to be brighter and crisper. He wants us to be more like him. Just as we look at pictures of our own Mother and Father and see the resemblance, God wants us to be more and more like him or Jesus when he walked this earth that is his, and our goal. When we come together with those thoughts, we give it all to him and accept him as our Lord and Savior and our world turns upside down. We are no longer what we used to be, freedom takes on a whole new meaning because He lives in us now, because the Holy Spirit has taken everything wrong, every word you've ever wanted to take back, everything that you know to be 'wrong and said to you, "I have taken it all away for you".

Read His story, that picture will develop in your mind and your emotions will race through you, the tears won't be of shame, they will turn into joy, uncontrollable joy. These tears will feel so good when you say Amen.

John 3:16–18 NIV 16. For God so loved the world that he gave his one and only Son, that whoever believes in him shall not perish but have eternal life. 17. For God did not send his Son into the world to condemn the world, but to save the world through him. 18. Whoever believes in him is not condemned, but whoever does not believe stands condemned already because they have not believed in the name of God's one and only Son.

This picture started over two thousand years ago and the family has grown, the Picture gets more beautiful every day! Can you imagine the size of that Family room, the size of that family Photo? Jesus said I go to prepare a place for you: John 14:1–4 1. "Do not let your hearts be troubled. You believe in God[a]; believe also in me. 2. My Father's house has many rooms; if that were not so, would I have told you that I am going there to prepare a place for you? 3. And if I go and prepare a place for you, I will come back and take you to be with me that you also may be where I am. 4. You know the way to the place where I am going." I believe this picture will be everlasting, and I don't think our Lord will be hanging this one on the wall. This picture will be a living, breathing and loving new life, 'all smiles, no rabbit ears, well maybe but I doubt it, and Jesus Christ will be beside all of us "all at once", in one shot.

He is with us now, but until we understand and believe the whole story, our vision is going to be blocked from seeing him and His wonders all around us. Our hearing and what he has been saying to us all of our lives but fail to hear over the noise of this three-dimensional body and single dimensional thinking.

Are you ready, you know "it has always been time" He has always been standing there waiting with open arms because He loves you unconditionally. Jesus Christ gives you a new purpose in Life and he's with you every step of the way. When you hear that song that touches your soul, when you hear those words from anywhere or anyone or you hear it on the radio, that's your Que. You're not in this place to make an impression. What purpose is embarrassment in an eternity? When you get to there you are either at Home plate or you've lost the game "No turning back", it's over.

Let go of that pew or seat in front of you, make your feet move, go to the alter and don't let that devil stop you! The Holy Spirit is whispering in your ear. Picture an eternity with the one who created you.

PLAN FOR THE FUTURE

Are saving up for the future? Are we working for a better life? The end of this world as we know it is coming to an end, Is it? If it is why do we worry about such things as where will our next meal come from what will we wear tomorrow where will we live? Matt. 6:30–32 NIV... 30. If that is how God clothes the grass of the field, which is here today and tomorrow is thrown into the fire, will he not much more clothe you—you of little faith? 31. So do not worry, saying, 'What shall we eat?' or 'What shall we drink?' or 'What shall we wear?' 32. For the pagans run after all these things, and your heavenly Father knows that you need them.

Are you a believer in God? Do you know what our Savior Jesus Christ did for you, me, everyone in this world and why? I know I know that's a lot of questions, so what's the point?

If you are worried about this world because it is going downhill in a landslide with all that has gone wrong, like uprisings in community, politics pushing for conformity to the will of every sin imaginable and making it the right that we know is wrong!

If you are planning for your eventual future? Think about this, what is more important after you are gone from this world? You do know it could happen at any time; the next minute, the next day, maybe next week. This is the one thing we should take care of because at the twinkling of an eye you could be facing heaven or hell. Instead of worrying about your life insurance policy what about the next time you open your eyes after your demise? I think that when we are close to death or have survived a near death moment, we have been given that chance, maybe your last chance to come to the Lord and say God please forgive me for my sins, I want to be with you when this life on earth is over. Thank you for sending your only son, our Savior Jesus Christ to us so that he can take our sins to a cross and die for. We also then know that on the third day he arose again.

Think about it the only sinless man that ever walked this earth taught us how we should live in a sin filled world and died for our sin because he loved us and wanted us to be with Him.

RUNNING OUT OF ROPE

Are you at the end of your rope? I was listening to Greg Laurie's daily Devotional and he was speaking of a businessman that started a lunchtime prayer meeting in 1857 at the North Dutch Church in New York. It is interesting to me that when the Stock market crashed the group grew from a handful to over fifty thousand people that came to the Lord. This reminded me of something that happened in 1990, 91 when our military were on the escapade to find Saddam Hussain. I was working in Ohio and also was in the Naval Reserves so we were a little on top of things as to civilians, "We had to pay attention to the news." Anyways someone approached me at work; he was a little nervous and asked me a question I wasn't quite ready for. He said, "Is this the end of the world?" I thought wow I never really gave it much thought but my kneejerk answer was; I'm not that worried about it because I know where I'm going if it is, he said where? Well," I'm going to heaven." He wanted to know more but he didn't want to talk to long about it right then he didn't have the time, I was getting ready to get off for the day and he had to go back to work. I remember telling him, we have had skirmishes like this before, but it sounded to a lot of people at that time, like it could be the big one!

1 Peter 3:5 NIV 15. But in your hearts revere Christ as Lord. Always be prepared to give an answer to everyone who asks you to give the reason for the hope that you have. But do this with gentleness and respect, well as most of you know Desert Storm only lasted

three months. Thinking about it now you would all be saying what a missed opportunity but it wasn't over yet the rest of the story makes all the difference. Before I left that day I asked a brother, believer in Christ to touch base with this man He needs the Lord and I think it's time. I know he followed through and as I remember it, he and his wife came to the Lord. All this hit me this morning I could just see people at the next big threat trying to hold on to that end of the rope before saying what can I lose? I know the story why did l, what am I waiting for. When we are at our ropes end, we don't always get the last word! What are you waiting for? By the way this revival from 1857 to 1859 became part of what is known as the Third Great Awakening in the United States. We must all be prepared for those that fear the Lord.

Mathew 24:6 NIV 6. You will hear of wars and rumors of wars, but see to it that you are not alarmed. Such things must happen, but the end is still to come.

THE UNSEEN

Analogy: A comparison between two things, typically for the purpose of explanation or clarification.

I am confused over the thought that there are people out there that don't believe in God. Some say it is because he is not visible or because they do not see his works being done!

When I read the Lutheran Hour Ministries lesson today the Lord spoke again to me about this. "Yes, the unseen Lord," the Holy Spirit. I have mentioned the obvious before: If you are educated in anything you can understand the reason for an analogy for it somewhere.

My simplest example comes from being an engineering minded person. It has always seemed to fit for an auto+ mechanic. But how about something even simpler; If you bought brand new batteries for a flashlight, and you change them out you would expect that flashlight to work, you would assume or trust that that flashlight will work; Why? How can, you be sure? You have developed a Faith in those batteries and the flashlight. When you plug in an appliance you might use it every day but you're sure it will work. You drive your car every day, you could've drove it a minute ago and you seriously believe it will start and run and take you wherever you want to go. That is faith without even blinking an eye!

You see the clouds, you feel the humidity, you see rain coming down 5 miles out, coming right toward you, "let me stop here for a second" I live in Arizona you can be right where I am describing and never get rain in this situation for some reason, God just must think

It has got to go somewhere else. It will stop within feet of where you are and you could step in and out of it or it will blow right around you. Anywhere else it would be there anything is possible with God, anything even rain in Arizona. Kidding, maybe ha ha.

Now some people believe in Heaven and Hell, some think there can be one and not the other! First off there can't be one without the other. When you were a kid did you ever get rewarded for something? Ice cream, stay up late let's not forget you can play your video games, (new to me, but then I have grandkids), and if you did something wrong and got caught there's the infamous "go to your room." The analogy? "Heaven or Hell" vs "Good or Bad." The only thing different here is with heaven you have to not just believe in Heaven and Hell you got to believe and accept Jesus Christ and what he has done to keep you out of hell. Jesus Christ who is God in the flesh came here for the reason that he loves all of his creation and after all the sacrifice throughout the Old Testament to compensate for sins, it was his last sacrifice of himself to take all the sin from whoever believes in him and throws the freewill that was given us out and choose to be with him after the end of our earthly life. He deserves our lives for what he did. There are so many things in this world we put our trust in, things we see and things we don't, how can anyone deny God and believe in tangibles. Do you remember what love felt like at first? Try to remember that and then multiply it by everyone in the world and then think about how Jesus feels when someone walks away from him. The bigger the body of Christ the more love he has for us.

THINGS ARE NOT ALWAYS WHAT THEY SEEM

Have you ever looked at an old beat-up car and thought, "man this thing isn't worth a second glance, it belongs in the scrap yard?" You walk past it with the thought "What a pile of junk" and then someone walks up and gets inside of it, starts the engine and you here it running like the smooth purr of a kitten! Then he puts it in 1 gear and it roars to life. What Just Happened? They call them sleepers; The Bodies of these cars are either made to look worse than they are or someone keeps the old body and builds up the undercarriage and drivetrain to that of a muscle car. Things are not always what they seem!

Our kids grew up kicking, screaming and complaining, they didn't want to do there chores, they wanted things we couldn't afford, they didn't like the food at times either. Funny thing, their friends would come over to play or do homework and we would "overhear every once in a while," the friends say something to the effect of "I wish we had parents like you got," or our kids would go to their friends house and we would get the "strangest comments" from their friends parents when we were at an outing together. "Your children are so well behaved!" Ok I am confused who's kids were they talking about, and where did "that" attitude go when they came back home? Things are not always what they seem!

2 Kings 6:14–17 NIV 14. Then he sent horses and chariots and a strong force there. They went by night and surrounded the city.

15. When the servant of the man of God got up and went out early the next morning, an army with horses and chariots had surrounded the city. "Oh no, my lord! What shall we do?" the servant asked.

16. "Don't be afraid," the prophet answered. "Those who are with us are more than those who are with them."

17. And Elisha prayed, "Open his eyes, Lord, so that he may see." Then the Lord opened the servant's eyes, and he looked and saw the hills full of horses and chariots of fire all around Elisha.

You see 'things are not always what they seem!" When you see the poor on the street, a scroungy man walking along the road, a young woman dressed in questionable attire, or a well- dressed guy in a fancy suit, we all need to ask the Lord to open our eyes through his heart. 1 Samuel 16:7b. NIV 7. But the Lord said to Samuel, "Do not consider his appearance or his height, for I have rejected him. The Lord does not look at the things people look at. People look at the outward appearance, but the Lord looks at the heart."

We need to cross that line, understand their story, reach out, lend a helping hand and introduce them to our Lord and Savior, only he can forgive their sins. We are all sinners, all of us," so we should never pass judgement on anyone. A lot of times things are not always what they seem" But our Lord and savior," He sees things just as they are".

TO BE OR NOT TO BE!

We have probably all heard these words written by Sir William Shakespeare but give no thought to their meaning, they are actually a pleading from Prince Hamlet over his life's troubles and what he should choose to do about them. I see another way for us to look at the question to be or not to be.

We all have these parts we have to play in our lives away from each other. Our jobs, maybe you serve the church while your significant other is serving somewhere else, maybe your spouse is serving overseas in the military while you are home with the family.

So, while you or your partner are away what do you always rely on, what is the one thing we can turn to, who is your strength when he or she is busy at that other place?

The promises of God run deep in you, "who belong to him." They run so deep at times that sometimes it is hard to know where God has taken up residence! Or God is in a shallow place in your soul always being ahead of the game where He should be in everything and everywhere you go. Let me put it another way, we get lazy and fall into the way we want to live, the things we want or want to do, that we just let His words, His ways sink so far back in our thinking that pretty soon you put him last, if you even remember Him, God has been dulled out. Or we have come to a realization that what we know to be Gods truth needs to be right up front where you can see Him in action and you not only want to be a part of Him you want others to be there with you.

So, when things start to look good to you and those things are trying to empower you, you recognize that it's not where you should go or be. That is the Holy Spirit telling you there is only one truth and one God to show you the way. So now we know what "SHOULD BE and what SHOULD NOT BE"

WE ARE ALL PRECIOUS STONES

There are 4 types of Facets for Gemstones

Crown
Pavillion
Table
Cutlet

Star Facet is another term that may refer to those bordering the Table Facets when they are designed to present a Star shape.

I have a hobby of finding rocks and taking them to a Hobby Shop called the AJ rock and gem club. We cut them and polish them and sometimes make jewelry out of them. We take an ugly rock and as we grind it down to a smoother finish it starts looking prettier because it shows us the different formations it has as we work it. Cut, Grind and Polish and then, the "Lapidarian" as they call us, can go a step further If we are really talented and schooled in it, we could facet it like most gem are for a ring or a broch or a really expensive necklace.

I thought about this as I contemplated the many hats we wear through life and how we sum up our lives. In my life I had a country boy upbringing, I went to church camp, school, this job that job, after all that I went to the Navy retired from there, I worked in a pottery making toilets, then we moved to Arizona where I took up a Job at a Defense company in production and then in Security and now retired but still working part time at a Home Depot.

Now I look at life like that ugly rock that has been cut, ground, shaped and polished and I am looking at all the facets and in those facets, there are those that shine and those that are tarnished those that didn't seem to polish out and I think over what Paul said in Philippians 4:11–13, NIV "11. I am not saying this because I am in need, for I have learned to be content whatever the circumstances. 12. I know what it is to be in need, and I know what it is to have plenty. I have learned the secret of being content in any and every situation, whether well fed or hungry, whether living in plenty or in want. 13. I can do all this through him who gives me strength.

From time to time I hurt over past mistakes and I feel it is a growing season, even though I have asked forgiveness for all my sins at the end of every day. I take it as a reminder that I must get even closer to our maker and sustainer, God and his son Jesus Christ who died on that cross and rose from the dead so that we will be with him in heaven.

When I start thinking this way the Holy Spirit reminds me of Philippians 3:12–14 12. Not that I have already obtained all this, or have already arrived at my goal, but I press on to take hold of that for which Christ Jesus took hold of me. 13. Brothers and sisters, I do not consider myself yet to have taken hold of it. But one thing I do: Forgetting what is behind and straining toward what is ahead, 14. I press on toward the goal to win the prize for which God has called me heavenward in Christ Jesus.

When I look at those dull beat-up nicked Facets in my life at different times in this life I look to what the Jeweler calls the "Table Facet" which is present in most Gems and is the largest flat area at the crown that presents the center of the Gem. I love this Analogy it seems to represent the difference between ourselves as we relate to Jesus Christ, God the Father God in the flesh.

WHAT ARE YOU GOOD AT

I got to thinking about the scriptures and how I used to know them better than I do now. Then my thoughts turned to who knows the scriptures better. Other than the Author's, "the disciple's," only God, Jesus and the Holy Spirit who gave the words to the disciples, to write the facts and what they were given through the trinity. They grew in the faith because they only knew two things, their own Jobs as fishermen, lawyer and Tent maker and this new path that took them away from they're old ways when Jesus chose them.

Now let's flip this around, what in your past, throughout your entire life is that one thing you learned so well that you cannot get the subject out of your mind, it was something you lived, breathed and were dedicated to for a long time? It could consume your conversations in social media and it captivates everything around you that reminds you of it. Those close to you that know you and remember it so well, that you actually vision yourself going to the same place and time and being able to do that job or hobby just as well as you did 20 yr.'s or even 50 yr.'s ago. It could be anything, Construction, working on cars, lawnmowers or it could be what you did during a 4yr. hitch in the service.

In conclusion, the disciples knew the scripture so well, why? Because they witnessed, lived, breathed, spoke and eventually wrote those words through the promptings of God. There are those out there that grew up reading, believing and living in the word, these could be the disciples of today, they know the Bible, the living word, because the words resonate in them like they did when the four gospels Mathew, Mark, Luke, John and others whose lives were so involved with the coming of, the living of, the crucifixion and the Glory of the resurrection of our Lord and Savior Jesus Christ for our sins.

When we live in the words as Jesus wants us to, the Holy Spirit moves you in such a way that you do not want look back. I have tasted a small morsel of this through the Holy Spirit. What is holding me back? What is holding you back? We believe but am not consumed in Him. Think back, what do you know that you were good at? The wakeup call is, "IT WAS ALL EARTHLY", all of it feels good to have learned and known, but because we belong to Him now or hopefully will soon in the near future, it will be part of his plan and He uses it for his glory then what is the gain in it. Paul said in Phil. 1:20–21 NIV, 20. I eagerly expect and hope that I will in no way be ashamed, but will have sufficient courage so that now as always Christ will be exalted in my body, whether by life or by death. 21. For to me, to live is Christ and to die is gain.

PART 6

SERVING

A SERVANT OF ALL

I put in for a lead Job two times that I remember and I didn't get it. I was a little hurt the first time but the second time I understood something that I learned from the Lord. I remember but he that is greatest among you shall be your servant. I don't think he meant to stop serving when you become a leader, but to know how to serve and that it is a tool that you will be able to pick up at just the right time when he needs you to.

So I want to be prepared all the time. Mark 9:34–35… 34. But they were silent, for on the way they had been arguing with each other which of them was the greatest. 35 Sitting down, Jesus called the Twelve and said, "If anyone wants to be first, and he must be the last of all and the servant of all."

I never forgot this; I was in a leading position of a Veterans Organization and I stopped in one morning to see how everyone was doing I noticed the snow had not been shoveled out at the entrance of the building We had hired someone to do this every morning before we opened up and Ed hadn't been there yet I went in and started asking what in the world was going on, I sat down at the bar and started asking the normal questions is he alright has anyone called him I wonder when he would get here and was worried that someone would hurt themselves on the walk way. Just then there was this guy, "Tony I think," that was drinking a beer He had no interest in my dilemma, but he was a friend He turned to me and said, "Why don't you do it?" His was just another voice out there. Then he said,

"Yea why sit around and complain about, just go out and do it your-self" I said "you know what, your right" so I went out and for about an hour I shoveled the side walk, and about the time I had finished Ed showed up Perfect timing ah yes it was but was it his or the Lords I would go with the latter of the two.

Matt. 23:8–12 NIV 8 "But you are not to be called 'Rabbi,' for you have one Teacher, and you are all brothers. 9 And do not call anyone on earth 'father,' for you have one Father, and he is in heaven. 10. Nor are you to be called instructors, for you have one Instructor, the Messiah. 11. The greatest among you will be your servant. 12. For those who exalt themselves will be humbled, and those who humble themselves will be exalted.

I should have figured out that the Lord had a plan from the start. There was a lesson there, I just had to listen, even if it came from a friend that didn't seem to care one way or another, God used him to show me to take the job of the servants even though I was a leader. I wasn't stepping down; I was stepping out. I didn't walk away I was walking through, God didn't say why I should do this; he was saying I am doing this because I love you, all of you!

ARE WE THERE YET?

While a lot of us feel it's wrong to ask questions of our God, Jesus and our existence to this world. I can relate to that at times. When we were young, we didn't get scolded for asking questions of our earthly Fathers. Are we there yet? What does this do? What happens when I do this?

In my day the worst thing a parent could do was make and act out the statement, "out of sight; out of mind" and "Do what I say, not as I do." That to me is real damage and hurtful damage.

2 Tim. 3:16–17 NIV says; 16. All Scripture is God-breathed and is useful for teaching, rebuking, correcting and training in righteousness, 17. So that the servant of God may be thoroughly equipped for every good work.

Why, would our heavenly father not understand questions that we have? He never got angry with Gideon when he wanted proof that who he was talking to was the real deal, how many times did he ask for that time and time again? I cringe every time I read that, It's like seeing a car accident in replay, you see what's coming but you still turn the other way, just like it's happening to you.

If you see someone from your past surprise you, what's the first thing you say? Is that really you? Myself when I have those kind 'a questions the first thing I do is say, and I feel like "I'm from Missouri,"

"SHOW ME!" and you know what? When he shows up, I am so glad I was bold enough to ask him. The things that he does to prove to me that he exists everywhere and, in my life, and my soul, be them small or large, I am so grateful and in awe of the way he goes out on a limb for me! I just want to go out and play dumb just to see what he will do next. I will Love my God, My Jesus, His Holy Spirit that he gave me more and more every day. I only have a little advice to anyone who sees an abnormal situation happen in front of them like oh say someone comes up to you totally out of the blue and asks you for a "particular" amount of money, usually it's a small amount; check your pockets before you walk away or say I don't have it. If you want to see the Lord at work count it out, you be so humbled that the exact amount just happens to be in your pocket or in your hand at the time that you met this person.

I have witnessed so many things like this, and brothers and sisters there is no coincident in my life it's all God. Don't turn away from the replay, don't walk past that person if you get the nudge and if someone asks you for something don't hesitate to check and see if the Lord has something in store for you, yes rea proof, you'll want to play dumb again and again, Bless me Lord but most of all Bless those you put in my path hopefully every day Amen.

HERO

At some point you will come to the realization that "Hero's" are everyday people that do not plan or realize those motives that we see in them until after they act without thought of themselves for others that cannot. At some point you will come to the realization that "Hero's" are everyday people that do not plan or realize those motives that we see in them until after they act without thought of themselves for others that cannot.

Rom. 5:6–11 NIV 6. You see, at just the right time, when we were still powerless, Christ died for the ungodly. 7. Very rarely will anyone die for a righteous person, though for a good person someone might possibly dare to die. 8. But God demonstrates his own love for us in this: While we were still sinners, Christ died for us.

9. Since we have now been justified by his blood, how much more shall we be saved from God's wrath through him! 10. For if, while we were God's enemies, we were reconciled to him through the death of his Son, how much more, having been reconciled, shall we be saved through his life! 11. Not only is this so, but we also boast in God through our Lord Jesus Christ, through whom we have now received reconciliation.

The only bona fide Hero in the History of the world, is the one who planned that event for the sake of the people of the world with the greatest sacrifice to himself even death on a cross, yes for the ones that he has always loved, yesterday, today and tomorrow.

OUR HEROES

We as young boys and girls watched the news, saw the wars and at the same time we saw the movies. We saw one of the most decorated Men in the Army "Audie Murphy" acting out his time in the military in a movie "To Hell and Back". That was a true story of his life during WWII. He then starred in some of the most popular westerns ever to hit the silver screen. That was one of our Hero's, of course there was John Wayne, William Lawrence Boyd or as some would remember him as, "Hop along Cassidy", Kirk Douglas, and Clint Eastwood. All the people we looked up to, all the movies we enjoyed. We picked up on the one liners the walk, stance and mannerisms of those characters and shows on the tv. At the same time we would see the news and think of following in our fathers and fore father's footsteps and fighting for our country.

There were and are a lot of young men and now young women joining the military and they get that "surprise" this is not like the movie's look on their faces! There isn't an audience out there for you. Now you've already committed yourself and the fine print says nothing about a swinging or revolving door policy, so you belong to the Army, Navy, Airforce, Marines or the Coast Guard for at least one hitch. Your way of life changes the second you leave the barber's chair, or when you're called to muster in front of your racks, or standing on what you now call a grinder. Then you start learning the swagger the rules and all the tools that look nothing like the hunting weapons or camping supplies you used to use. Your mother and father will only recognize your letters and an occasional phone call if you're lucky. Your CC or CO has put the definition into your heads, "we" are now your parents and forgetting to pick up after yourself will indeed lead to punishment the likes your real parents never had in mind and this time you won't get away with saying I don't want to.

You will come out a better person with bad habits that are hard to break and if Church was a part of you before and has slipped your mind or heart, you will sooner or later remember what God meant to us all when he sent his son to this earth to die for our sins and you will be back in his loving arms again.

If you were to ask a service member, "A VET", what they did when they were in, you will most likely hear them say, if they will even talk about it at all, "I did my job". The service will make a man or a woman out of you some will become broken for some reason or another and some will be noticeably broken physically or mentally. They will never be that kid on the farm or the one that went out with you on a date. They will have to spill their guts about everything that went on, to God and then their spouse at one time or another and our God will, as always be there every step of the way. When we get to that point, he is standing there just like he was all through our lives and yes that means all through the good times and bad.

You know I hear a lot of people that were in the service, make this one mistake and I correct them, "I have to!" They say "I was an X Sailor, X Marine, X Army, X Airforce or X Coast Guard." Truth is once you were in the service you are not an "X" anything, you were there, doesn't matter what you did, doesn't matter that you were in for two or twenty, good, bad or indifferent and It is the same with the promise of our Lord Jesus Christ once you have accepted him as your savior you are never an "X Christian" not for a day, not for an eternity.

At some point you will come to the realization that "Hero's" are everyday people that do not plan or realize those motives that we see in them until after they act without thought for others that cannot. That is the gift of the Holy Spirit that moves in them as he does in everyone.

The only bona fide Hero in the History of the world, is the one who planned that event for the sake of the people of the world with the greatest sacrifice to himself, even death on a cross, yes for the ones that he has always loved, yesterday, today and tomorrow!

WHAT WE HAVE BECOME BECAUSE OF OUR FATHER'S

John 14:8–14 NIV 8. Philip said, "Lord, show us the Father and that will be enough for us." 9. Jesus answered: "Don't you know me, Philip, even after I have been among you such a long time? Anyone who has seen me has seen the Father. How can you say, 'Show us the Father'? 10. Don't you believe that I am in the Father, and that the Father is in me? The words I say to you I do not speak on my own authority. Rather, it is the Father, living in me, who is doing his work. 11. Believe me when I say that I am in the Father and the Father is in me; or at least believe on the evidence of the works themselves. 12. Very truly I tell you, whoever believes in me will do the works I have been doing, and they will do even greater things than these, because I am going to the Father. 13. And I will do whatever you ask in my name, so that the Father may be glorified in the Son. 14. You may ask me for anything in my name, and I will do it.

A lot of us grow up with fathers we are proud of and it seems to me we try our darndest to impress our dad's all of our lives in everything we do. It seems like it's not important to Him but we just keep on trying to outdo what our fathers do. With Jesus it is made known that that trait is built in us for a reason it just takes time, prayer and reading the good book to figure out why.

1 John 2:5–8 (NIV) 5. But if anyone obeys his word, love for God is truly mode complete in them. This is how we know we ore in him: 6. whoever claims to live in him must live as Jesus did. 7. Dear friends, I am not writing you a new command but on old one, which you have had since the beginning, this old command is the message you have heard. 8. Yet I am writing you a new command; its truth is seen in him and in you, because the darkness is passing and the true light is already shining. I am Grateful to have had a dad that taught me a lot about who I have become today But also for my Father in Heaven who never stops teaching me of who and what I will become and what I will attain for his Kingdom, "our Kingdom," before I am with Him in Heaven for an Eternity. God Bless all you fathers out there!

WHERE IS CHURCH WHEN YOU ARE NOT HOME

When my son was in the military, he contacted me and he said he felt guilty that he could never find time to go to church (they had him flying and monitoring the systems of the plane). I told him the church is not a building the church is you. Pray on what you know of the Bible and the Holy Spirit will help you through these times.

I wish I could have had this story that will assist anyone who ever knew or knows the Bible to glorify Him not only to themselves but others. When you think you are all alone, think about this story and maybe, carry around a deck of cards.

It was quiet that day, the guns and the mortars and land mines for some reason hadn't been heard. The young soldier knew it was Sunday, the holiest day of the week. As he was sitting there, he got out an old deck of cards and laid them out across his bunk. Just then an Army sergeant came in and said, why aren't you with the rest of your platoon? The soldier replied, "I thought I would stay behind and spend some time with the Lord." The sergeant said, Look's to me like you're going to play cards." The soldier said, "No sir. You see, since we are not allowed to have Bibles or other spiritual books in this country, I've decided to talk to the Lord by studying this deck of cards." The sergeant asked in disbelief, "How will you do that?"

You see the Ace, Sergeant? It reminds me that there is only one God. The two represents the two parts of the Bible, Old and New testaments. The three represents the Father the son and the Holy Ghost. The four stands for the Four Gospels: Matthew, Mark, Luke and John. The Five is for the five virgins that were ten but only five were glorified. The six is for the six days it took God to create the Heavens and the Earth. The Seven is for the day God rested and making His Creation. The eight is for the family of Noah and his wife, their three sons and their wives- the eight people God spared from the flood that destroyed the earth. The Nine is for the lepers that Jesus cleansed of leprosy. He cleansed ten, but nine never thanked Him. The Ten represents the Ten Commandments that God handed down to Moses on tablets of stone. The Jack is a reminder of Satan, on of God's first angels, but he got kicked out of heaven for his sly and wicked ways and now he is the joker of eternal hell. The queen stands for the Virgin Mary. The King stands for Jesus, for he is the King of all Kings. When I count all the dots on all I the cards, I come up with 375 total, one for every day of the year. There are a total of 52 cards in a deck; each is a week- 52 week in a year. The four suits represent the four seasons: Spring, summer, fall and winter. Each suit has thirteen cards- there are exactly thirteen weeks in a quarter. So when I want to talk to God and thank Him, I just pull out this old deck of cards and they remind me of all that I have to be thankful for. The sergeant just stood there. After a minute, with tears in his eyes and pain in his heart, he said, "Soldier, can I borrow that deck of cards?" I do not know the author of this RJH II.

WHO OR WHAT IS A CHURCH?

Some say the church means one thing and some make it out to be something else, they say they don't need to go to a building that some do consider the Church. I've been told by some that their Church is alone time at their favorite fishing Hole. Some have said its out on a hill or mountain side taking in the beauty of the outdoors and some say they get their advice or wisdom from a bartender or from sitting in a barber's chair. I make it a point to never condemn or convict anyone, it's not my job, I do however like to talk about their thought on God or whatever they believe God to be. I like to talk about the ways of our heart and soul, but I really love to listen even more. I feel that about three quarters of people's problems are usually solved if we just sit and keep our mouths shut and let them get things off their minds.

Perhaps I or we as followers of Jesus Christ should be asking what the Lord has been feeding or speaking to them while they are in whatever their church is to them. Romans 16:5 (NIV) 5. Greet also the church that meets at their house. Greet my dear friend Epenetus, who was the first convert to Christ in the province of Asia.

We all have stories about church some are why they turned away from that building which is the gathering of the Body of Christ, and sometimes it's some small thing like a job they just can't get off away from on days that the church is gathering. We are his Body of believers, we need to make that grow, and that is our purpose as followers of His. Eph. 1:22–23 (NIV) 22. And God placed all things under his feet and appointed him to be head over everything for the church, 23. which is His body, the fullness of him who fills everything in every way.

You can put a label on it like a lot of people that call their church by another name. If we were all to sit down and discuss our stories our ideas on what the Church is, or should be. I think it would be a very interesting conversation, and I would have to say that each and every one of us would have a similar view of just what we believe the church really is. We all know it is a sanctuary in some respect or another. Galatians 1:1–2 1. Paul, an apostle—sent not from men nor by a man, but by Jesus Christ and God the Father, who raised him from the dead 2. and all the brothers and sisters with me.

YOU AND ME GOD

My tank is about empty, the time I need to get to work is getting short, my car is a little older and not in the best of shape, it has to make it.

Patience is a virtue; it's also something we lack. Do we ask too much of the Lord? I think we do when we demand it like we want it "right now." Not that we shouldn't ask anyways and if the Lord our God thinks it's important to have it "right now" then he would move Heaven and Hell to get it there, "literally."

Instead of wasting our energy worrying about what may become of all those things that we do not have control over why not put it in the hands of the Lord and trust in God for all those things that you worry about Just as we were taught through the Bible.

If your friends, family, neighbors and coworkers are struggling for anything they need or want, be it health, a car to run right, something that needs fixed, bills and so on; it's time to let your light shine through. They need to see Christ in you and we need to be ready to explain how you received that light and how reassuring it is to hand all your problems and all your wants and needs to Him.

So, when you start thinking things are impossible remember Matt. 19:26 Jesus looked at them and said, "with man this is impossible, but with God all things are possible... By the way my wife stopped me from going to the gas station on the way to work she said He would get me there and back you know what, it had bounced off empty all morning until I started to work from where she said that and all the way to work it showed a quarter tank imagine that, God runs a gas station too.

John 14:13–14 NIV 13. And I will do whatever you ask in my name, so that the Father may be glorified in the Son. 14. You may ask me for anything in my name, and I will do it.

WHAT GOD IS THAT PERFECT WORD

Lord as the mist rolls out of the grass and drifts away,
I ask you Father to show me this new day.
With pen in hand and eyes on you,
I pray lord gift me with words lived through,
For in no way do I live a perfect life,
These hours of beauty are with me in strife.
Grant me father words to other sinners, your truth,
Show them your way, your words that sooth.
For what dear God is your perfect word that be,
That will bring all souls into loves eternity.
For why is your love, that we search for, to find, so hard,
When so closely to our souls you guard.
Free will you gave but our love is all you ever asked,
For this you sent your Son who like the fisherman's line you cast.
The living Story that is in your book be told,
Of your son Jesus whose truth given, is so bold.
Gave us those words, healing and much more,
After years of offering up sacrifice from before.
Our Jesus had the answer all along,
To suffer and die on a cross for all our wrong.
All proof that Gods Love conquers all,

In three days his body had left the tomb as was his call.
For we now have proof of His promise and it is here,
We only need to believe in Jesus, ask forgiveness and then there is
no fear.

We know now God is three in one,
He is the father and then the spirit and Jesus the son.

YFICA

HOW MANY TIMES HAVE I TOLD YOU?

How many times do we have to be told something before it sets in? How many times do we tell our children no? Always having to remind them throughout the day of things like chores, you know dishes, mowing the lawn or their homework!

How many times or ways to explain what they better do before they cannot weasel their way from what exactly the order is?

Sometimes as parents you almost feel like you have to be a lawyer to get your point across. Children will cross examine everything you say to make it come out, to what they want it to mean; Am I right?

I thought about the analogy of this versus how many times the Lord has been tested by us versus the early ones of the Bible that we do things correctly. For instance, Moses and the burning bush for an attention getter. He already got his attention yet Moses tested the Lord by saying I am slow of speech and tongue in Exodus 4:10–12.

Gideon testing the Lord more than once in judges 6:17 After an Angel of the Lord appears to him and called on this farmer of a clan that is the weakest of Manasseh a mighty Warrior where he says:

If now I have found favor in your eyes, give me a sign that it is really you talking to me. It goes on, but the point I am making is this, just like children that question their parents we do the same with God.

So, how many times has the Lord said I love you? How many times in the Bible has it been pointed out to us through scriptures from Gods heart? How many times has Jesus explained to us not only his purpose of the same, but the only way that he could do that by becoming the last sacrifice for us, by taking all our sin of all time from us to the cross.

Here is a list I looked up, I count a hundred. How many times has he asked you to do this and did you listen?

This is the message, John 3:16 "For God so loved the world, that he gave his only Son, that whoever believes in him should not perish but have eternal life.

THIS was a CHRISTMAS message but it is for all times: SPREAD THE WORD, HOW MANY TIMES HAS GOD / JESUS / THROUGH THE HOLY SPIRIT SAID TO "YOU:" I LOVE YOU AND WANT TO BE WITH YOU UNTIL THE END OF TIME AND ETERNITY. Are you listening? Do you believe?

Romans 10:9–10 NIV 9. If you declare with your mouth, "Jesus is Lord," and believe in your heart that God raised him from the dead, you will be saved. 10. For it is with your heart that you believe and are justified, and it is with your mouth that you profess your faith and are saved.

John 3:16 NIV 16. For God so loved the world that he gave his one and only Son, that whoever believes in him shall not perish but have eternal life.

Ephesians 2:8–10 NIV 8. For it is by grace you have been saved, through faith—and this is not from yourselves, it is the gift of God—9. Not by works, so that no one can boast. 10. For we are God's handiwork, created in Christ Jesus to do good works, which God prepared in advance for us to do.

Works, which God prepared beforehand, that we should walk in them.

Romans 10:13 NIV 13. "For everyone who calls on the name of the Lord will be saved."

John 3:5 NIV 5. Jesus answered, "Very truly I tell you, no one can enter the kingdom of God unless they are born of water and the Spirit.

Romans 6:23 NIV 23. For the wages of sin is death, but the gift of God is eternal life in Christ Jesus our Lord.

Romans 3:23 NIV 23. for all have sinned and fall short of the glory of God,

Acts 2:38, 39 NIV 38. Peter replied, "Repent and be baptized, every one of you, in the name of Jesus Christ for the forgiveness of your sins. And you will receive the gift of the Holy Spirit. 39. The promise is for you and your children and for all who are far off—for all whom the Lord our God will call."

* James 2:14–25 NIV 14. What good is it, my brothers and sisters, if someone claims to have faith but has no deeds? Can such faith save them? 15. Suppose a brother or a sister is without clothes and daily food. 16. If one of you says to them, "Go in peace; keep warm and well fed," but does nothing about their physical needs, what good is it? 17. In the same way, faith by itself, if it is not accompanied by action, is dead. 18. But someone will say, "You have faith; I have deeds."

Show me your faith without deeds, and I will show you my faith by my deeds. 19. You believe that there is one God. Good! Even the demons believe that—and shudder.

20. You foolish person, do you want evidence that faith without deeds is useless? 21. was not our father Abraham considered righteous for what he did when he offered his son Isaac on the altar? 22. You see that his faith and his actions were working together, and his faith was made complete by what he did. 23. And the scripture was fulfilled that says, "Abraham believed God, and it was credited to him as righteousness," and he was called God's friend. 24. You see that a person is considered righteous by what they do and not by faith alone.

25. In the same way, was not even Rahab the prostitute considered righteous for what she did when she gave lodging to the spies and sent them off in a different direction?

Acts 22:16 NIV And now what are you waiting for? Get up, be baptized and wash your sins away, calling on his name.

Acts 16:30–31 NIV 30. He then brought them out and asked, "Sirs, what must I do to be saved?"

31. They replied, "Believe in the Lord Jesus, and you will be saved—you and your household."

Mark '16:16 NIV whoever believes and is baptized will be saved, but whoever does not believe will be condemned.

Acts 2:38 NIV Peter replied, "Repent and be baptized, every one of you, in the name of Jesus Christ for the forgiveness of your sins. And you will receive the gift of the Holy Spirit.

1 John 5:13 NIV I write these things to you who believe in the name of the Son of God that you may know that you have eternal life.

Ephesians 2:8–9 NIV 8. For it is by grace you have been saved, through faith—and this is not from yourselves, it is the gift of God 9. Not by works, so that no one can boast.

Acts 16:31 NIV they replied, "Believe in the Lord Jesus, and you will be saved—you and your household."

1 John 1:9 NIV If we confess our sins, he is faithful and just and will forgive us our sins and purify us from all unrighteousness.

John 20:19–24 NIV 19. On the evening of that first day of the week, when the disciples were together, with the doors locked for fear of the Jewish leaders, Jesus came and stood among them and said, "Peace be with you!" 20. After he said this, he showed them his hands and side. The disciples were overjoyed when they saw the Lord.

21. Again Jesus said, "Peace be with you! As the Father has sent me, I am sending you." 22. And with that he breathed on them and said, "Receive the Holy Spirit. 23. If you forgive anyone's sins, their sins are forgiven; if you do not forgive them, they are not forgiven."

24. Now Thomas (also known as Didymus[a]), one of the Twelve, was not with the disciples when Jesus came.

1 Peter 3:18–22 NIV 18. For Christ also suffered once for sins, the righteous for the unrighteous, to bring you to God. He was put to death in the body but made alive in the Spirit. 19. After being made alive, he went and made proclamation to the imprisoned spirits—20. To those who were disobedient long ago when God waited patiently in the days of Noah while the ark was being built. In it only a few people, eight in all, were saved through water, 21. And this water symbolizes baptism that now saves you also—not the removal of dirt from the body but the pledge of a clear conscience toward

God. It saves you by the resurrection of Jesus Christ, 22. Who has gone into heaven and is at God's right hand—with angels, authorities and powers in submission to him.

Matthew 7:13–14 NIV 13. "Enter through the narrow gate. For wide is the gate and broad is the road that leads to destruction, and many enter through it. 14. But small is the gate and narrow the road that leads to life, and only a few find it.

Ephesians 2:10 NIV 10. For we are God's handiwork, created in Christ Jesus to do good works, which God prepared in advance for us to do.

Acts 4:12 NIV 12. Salvation is found in no one else, for there is no other name under heaven given to mankind by which we must be saved."

John '14:6 NIV 6. Jesus answered, "I am the way and the truth and the life. No one comes to the Father except through me.

Romans 2:16 NIV 16. This will take place on the day when God judges people's secrets through Jesus Christ, as my gospel declares.

John 3:19–21 NIV 19. This is the verdict: Light has come into the world, but people loved darkness instead of light because their deeds were evil. 20. Everyone who does evil hates the light, and will not come into the light for fear that their deeds will be exposed. 21. But whoever lives by the truth comes into the light, so that it may be seen plainly that what they have done has been done in the sight of God.

John 1:12 NIV 12. Yet to all who did receive him, to those who believed in his name, he gave the right to become children of God—

Hebrews 7:25 NIV 25. Therefore he is able to save completely those who come to God through him, because he always lives to intercede for them.

Ephesians 2:8 NIV 8. For it is by grace you have been saved, through faith—and this is not from yourselves, it is the gift of God—

Acts 2:41 NIV 41. Those who accepted his message were baptized, and about three thousand were added to their number that day.

John 5:24 NIV 24."Very truly I tell you, whoever hears my word and believes him who sent me has eternal life and will not be judged but has crossed over from death to life.

Matthew 7:21–23 NIV 21. "Not everyone who says to me, 'Lord, Lord,' will enter the kingdom of heaven, but only the one who does the will of my Father who is in heaven. 22. Many will say to me on that day, 'Lord, Lord, did we not prophesy in your name and in your name drive out demons and in your name perform many miracles?' 23. Then I will tell them plainly, 'I never knew you. Away from me, you evildoers!'

Romans 10:9 NIV 9. If you declare with your mouth, "Jesus is Lord," and believe in your heart that God raised him from the dead, you will be saved.

John 3:22–26 NIV 22. After this, Jesus and his disciples went out into the Judean countryside, where he spent some time with them, and baptized. 23. Now John also was baptizing at Aenon near Salim, because there was plenty of water, and people were coming and being baptized. 24. (This was before John was put in prison.) 25. An argument developed between some of John's disciples and a certain Jew over the matter of ceremonial washing. 26. They came to John and said to him, "Rabbi, that man who was with you on the other side of the Jordan—the one you testified about—look, he is baptizing, and everyone is going to him."

Timothy 2:15 NIV 15. Do your best to present yourself to God as one approved, a worker who does not need to be ashamed and who correctly handles the word of truth.

John 6:47 NIV 47. Very truly I tell you, the one who believes has eternal life.

Luke 19:10 NIV 10. For the Son of Man came to seek and to save the lost."

1 Timothy 2:4 NIV 4. Who wants all people to be saved and to come to a knowledge of the truth?

Acts 2:21 NIV 21. And everyone who calls on the name of the Lord will be saved.

John 6:55–59 NIV 55. For my flesh is real food and my blood is real drink. 56. Whoever eats my flesh and drinks my blood remains in me, and I in them. 57. Just as the living Father sent me and I live because of the Father, so the one who feeds on me will live because of me. 58. This is the bread that came down from heaven. Your ancestors ate manna and died, but whoever feeds on this bread will live forever." 59. He said this while teaching in the synagogue in Capernaum.

Matthew 1:21 NIV 21. She will give birth to a son, and you are to give him the name Jesus,[a] because he will save his people from their sins."

1 John 5:3 NIV 3. In fact, this is love for God: to keep his commands. And his commands are not burdensome,

2 Peter 3:9 NIV 9. The Lord is not slow in keeping his promise, as some understand slowness. Instead, he is patient with you, not wanting anyone to perish, but everyone to come to repentance.

1 Corinthians 15:1–4 NIV 1. Now, brothers and sisters, I want to remind you of the gospel I preached to you, which you received and on which you have taken your stand. 2. By this gospel you are saved, if you hold firmly to the word I preached to you. Otherwise, you have believed in vain.

3. For what I received I passed on to you as of first importance that Christ died for our sins according to the Scriptures, 4. That he was buried, that he was raised on the third day according to the Scriptures,

Acts 16:30 NIV 30. He then brought them out and asked, "Sirs, what must I do to be saved?"

John 6:65 NIV 65. He went on to say, "This is why I told you that no one can come to me unless the Father has enabled them."

Psalm 1:1–6 NIV 1. Blessed is the one who does not walk in step with the wicked or stand in the way that sinners take more sit in the company of mockers, 2. Whose delight is in the law of the Lord, and who meditates on his law day and night. 3. That person is like a tree planted by streams of water, which yields its fruit in season and whose leaf does not wither—whatever they do prospers. 4. Not so the wicked! They are like chaff that the wind blows away. 5. Therefore the wicked will not stand in the judgment, nor sinners in the assembly of the righteous. 6. For the Lord watches over the way of the righteous, but the way of the wicked leads to destruction.

1 Corinthians 1:18 NIV 18. For the message of the cross is foolishness to those who are perishing, but to us who are being saved it is the power of God.

Romans 2:6–8 NIV 6. God "will repay each person according to what they have done." 7. To those who by persistence in doing good seek glory, honor and immortality, he will give eternal life. 8. But for those who are self-seeking and who reject the truth and follow evil, there will be wrath and anger.

Romans 1:16 NIV 16. For I am not ashamed of the gospel, because it is the power of God that brings salvation to everyone who believes: first to the Jew, then to the Gentile.

John 11:25–26 NIV 25. Jesus said to her, "I am the resurrection and the life. The one who believes in me will live, even though they die; 26. and whoever lives by believing in me will never die. Do you believe this?"

John 3:36 NIV 36. Whoever believes in the Son has eternal life, but whoever rejects the Son will not see life, for God's wrath remains on them.

John 3:3 NIV 3. Jesus replied, "Very truly I tell you, no one can see the kingdom of God unless they are born again.

Luke 13:3 NIV 3. I tell you, no! But unless you repent, you too will all perish.

Mark 1:15 NIV 15. "The time has come," he said. "The kingdom of God has come near. Repent and believe the good news!"

Matthew 25:31–40 NIV 31. "When the Son of Man comes in his glory, and all the angels with him, he will sit on his glorious throne. 32. All the nations will be gathered before him, and he will separate the people one from another as a shepherd separates the sheep from the goats. 33. He will put the sheep on his right and the goats on his left.

34. "Then the King will say to those on his right, 'Come, you who are blessed by my Father; take your inheritance, the kingdom prepared for you since the creation of the world. 35. For I was hungry and you gave me something to eat, I was thirsty and you gave me something to drink, I was a stranger and you invited me in, 36. I

needed clothes and you clothed me, I was sick and you looked after me, I was in prison and you came to visit me.'

37. "Then the righteous will answer him, 'Lord, when did we see you hungry and feed you, or thirsty and give you something to drink? 38. When did we see you a stranger and invite you in, or needing clothes and clothe you? 39. When did we see you sick or in prison and go to visit you?'

40. "The King will reply, 'Truly I tell you, whatever you did for one of the least of these brothers and sisters of mine, you did for me.'

John 6:44 NIV No one can come to me unless the Father who sent me draws him. And I will raise him up on the last day.

John 3:16–17 NIV 16. For God so loved the world that he gave his one and only Son, that whoever believes in him shall not perish but have eternal life. 17. For God did not send his Son into the world to condemn the world, but to save the world through him.

Titus 3:5 NIV 5. He saved us, not because of righteous things we had done, but because of his mercy. He saved us through the washing of rebirth and renewal by the Holy Spirit,

2 Corinthians 5:21 NIV 21. God made him who had no sin to be sin for us, so that in him we might become the righteousness of God.

Romans 10:10 NIV 10. For it is with your heart that you believe and are justified, and it is with your mouth that you profess your faith and are saved.

Romans 3:8 NIV 8. Why not say—as some slanderously claim that we say—"Let us do evil that good may result"? Their condemnation is just!

John 6:67–71 NIV 67. "You do not want to leave too, do you?" Jesus asked the Twelve.

68. Simon Peter answered him, "Lord, to whom we shall go? You have the words of eternal life. 69. We have come to believe and to know that you are the Holy One of God."

70. Then Jesus replied, "Have I not chosen you, the Twelve? Yet one of you is a devil!" **71** (He meant Judas, the son of Simon Iscariot, who, though one of the Twelve, was later to betray him.).

John 6:28–29 NIV 28. Then they asked him, "What must we do to do the works God requires?"

29. Jesus answered, "The work of God is this: to believe in the one he has sent."

Mark 16:15–16 NIV 15. He said to them, "Go into the entire world and preach the gospel to all creation. **16** Whoever believes and is baptized will be saved, but whoever does not believe will be condemned.

Hebrews 6:4–6 NIV 4. It is impossible for those who have once been enlightened, who have tasted the heavenly gift, who have shared in the Holy Spirit, 5. who have tasted the goodness of the word of God and the powers of the coming age 6. And who have fallen[a] away, to be brought back to repentance. To their loss they are crucifying the Son of God all over again and subjecting him to public disgrace.

Acts 3:19 NIV 19. Repent, then, and turn to God, so that your sins may be wiped out, that times of refreshing may come from the Lord,

John 6:40 NIV F40. Or my Father's will is that everyone who looks to the Son and believes in him shall have eternal life, and I will raise them up at the last day."

Hebrews 10:26 NIV 26. If we deliberately keep on sinning after we have received the knowledge of the truth, no sacrifice for sins is left,

Ephesians 1:13–14 NIV 13. And you also were included in Christ when you heard the message of truth, the gospel of your salvation. When you believed, you were marked in him with a seal, the promised Holy Spirit, 14. Who is a deposit guaranteeing our inheritance until the redemption of those who are God's possession—to the praise of his glory.

Romans 10:1–5 "read on to" 21 NIV 1. Brothers and sisters, my heart's desire and prayed to God for the Israelites is that they may be saved. 2. For I can testify about them that they are zealous for God, but their zeal is not based on knowledge. 3. Since they did not know the righteousness of God and sought to establish their own, they did not submit to God's righteousness. 4. Christ is the culmination of the law so that there may be righteousness for everyone who believes.

5. Moses writes this about the righteousness that is by the law: "The person who does these things will live by them.

Romans 6:1–7 NIV 1. What shall we say, then? Shall we go on sinning so that grace may increase? 2. By no means! We are those who have died to sin; how can we live in it any longer? 3. Or don't you know that all of us who were baptized into Christ Jesus were baptized into his death? 4. We were therefore buried with him through baptism into death in order that, just as Christ was raised from the dead through the glory of the Father, we too may live a new life.

5. For if we have been united with him in a death like his, we will certainly also be united with him in a resurrection like his. 6. For we know that our old self was crucified with him so that the body ruled by sin might be done away with, that we should no longer be slaves to sin—7. Because anyone who has died has been set free from sin.

What shall we say then? Are we to continue in sin that grace may abound? By no means! How can we who died to sin still live in it? Do you not know that all of us who have been baptized into Christ Jesus were baptized into his death? We were buried therefore with him by baptism into death, in order that, just as Christ was raised from the dead by the glory of the Father, we too might walk in newness of life. For if we have been united with him in a death like his, we shall certainly be united with him in a resurrection like his....

Acts 2:1–6 NIV 1. When the day of Pentecost came, they were all together in one place. 2. Suddenly a sound like the blowing of a violent wind came from heaven and filled the whole house where they were sitting. 3. They saw what seemed to be tongues of fire that separated and came to rest on each of them. 4. All of them were filled with the Holy Spirit and began to speak in other tongues as the Spirit enabled them.

5. Now there were staying in Jerusalem God-fearing Jews from every nation under heaven. 6. When they heard this sound, a crowd came together in bewilderment, because each one heard their own language being spoken.

John 14:12 NIV 12. Very truly I tell you, whoever believes in me will do the works I have been doing, and they will do even greater things than these, because I am going to the Father.

Matthew 5:48 NIV 48. Be perfect, therefore, as your heavenly Father is perfect.

2 Timothy 1:9 NIV 9. He has saved us and called us to a holy life—not because of anything we have done but because of his own purpose and grace. This grace was given us in Christ Jesus before the beginning of time.

2 Corinthians 7:10 NIV 10. Godly sorrow brings repentance that leads to salvation and leaves no regret, but worldly sorrow brings death.

1 Corinthians 12:12–13 NIV 12. Just as a body, though one, has many parts, but all its many parts form one body, so it is with Christ. 13. For we were all baptized by[a] one Spirit so as to form one body—whether Jews or Gentiles, slave or free—and we were all given the one Spirit to drink.

Romans 5:8 NIV 8. But God demonstrates his own love for us in this: While we were still sinners, Christ died for us.

Acts 17:30 NIV 30. In the past God overlooked such ignorance, but now he commands all people everywhere to repent.

Acts 13:47 NIV 47. For this is what the Lord has commanded us: 'I have made you a light for the Gentiles, that you may bring salvation to the ends of the earth.

Matthew '16:18 NIV 18. And I tell you that you are Peter, and on this rock I will build my church, and the gates of Hades will not overcome it.

Isaiah 53:1–12 NIV 1. Who has believed our message and to whom has the arm of the Lord been revealed? 2. He grew up before him like a tender shoot, and like a root out of dry ground.

He had no beauty or majesty to attract us to him, nothing in his appearance that we should desire him.

3. He was despised and rejected by mankind, a man of suffering, and familiar with pain.

Like one from whom people hide their faces he was despised, and we held him in low esteem.

4. Surely, he took up our pain and bore our suffering, yet we considered him punished by God, stricken by him, and afflicted.

5. But he was pierced for our transgressions, he was crushed for our iniquities; the punishment that brought us peace was on him, and by his wounds we are healed.

6. We all, like sheep, have gone astray, each of us has turned to our own way; and the Lord has laid on him the iniquity of us all. 7. He was oppressed and afflicted, yet he did not open his mouth;

He was led like a lamb to the slaughter, and as a sheep before its shearers is silent, so he did not open his mouth. 8. By oppression and judgment he was taken away. Yet who of his generation protested?

For he was cut off from the land of the living; for the transgression of my people, he was punished.

9. He was assigned a grave with the wicked, and with the rich in his death, though he had done no violence, nor was any deceit in his mouth. 10. Yet it was the Lord's will to crush him and cause him to suffer, and though the Lord makes his life an offering for sin, he will see his offspring and prolong his days, and the will of the Lord will prosper in his hand. 11. After he has suffered, he will see the light of life and be satisfied; by his knowledge my righteous servant will justify many, and he will bear their iniquities. 12. Therefore I will give him a portion among the great, and he will divide the spoils with the strong, because he poured out his life unto death, and was numbered with the transgressors. For he bore the sin of many, and made intercession for the transgressors.

Revelation 20:11–15 NIV 11. Then I saw a great white throne and him who was seated on it. The earth and the heavens fled from his presence, and there was no place for them. 12. And I saw the dead, great and small, standing before the throne, and books were opened. Another book was opened, which is the book of life. The dead were judged according to what they had done as recorded in the books. 13. The sea gave up the dead that were in it, and death and Hades gave up the dead that were in them, and each person was judged according to what they had done. 14. Then death and Hades were thrown into the lake of fire. The lake of fire is the second death.

15. Anyone whose name was not found written in the book of life was thrown into the lake of fire.

Hebrews 9:28 NIV 28. So, Christ was sacrificed once to take away the sins of many; and he will appear a second time, not to bear sin, but to bring salvation to those who are waiting for him.

Mark 10:17–21 NIV 17. As Jesus started on his way, a man ran up to him and fell on his knees before him. "Good teacher," he asked, "what must I do to inherit eternal life?"

18. "Why do you call me good?" Jesus answered. "No one is good—except God alone. 19. You know the commandments: 'You shall not murder, you shall not commit adultery, you shall not steal, you shall not give false testimony, you shall not defraud, honor your father and mother.'"

20. "Teacher," he declared, "all these I have kept since I was a boy."

21. Jesus looked at him and loved him. "One thing you lack," he said. "Go, sell everything you have and give to the poor, and you will have treasure in heaven. Then come, follow me."

Psalm 62:1 NIV 1. Truly my soul finds rest in God; my salvation comes from him.

Revelation 3:20 NIV 20. Behold, I stand at the door and knock. If anyone hears my voice and opens the door, I will come in to him and eat with him, and he with me.

Revelation 1:1–5 NIV 1. The revelation from Jesus Christ, which God gave him to show his servants what must soon take place. He made it known by sending his angel to his servant John, 2. Who testifies to everything he saw—that is, the word of God and the testimony of Jesus Christ. 3. Blessed is the one who reads aloud the words of this prophecy, and blessed are those who hear it and take to heart what is written in it, because the time is near. 4. John, to the seven churches in the province of Asia:

Grace and peace to you from him who is, and who was, and who is to come, and from the seven spirits before his throne, 5. And from Jesus Christ, who is the faithful witness, the firstborn from the dead, and the ruler of the kings of the earth.

To him who loves us and has freed us from our sins by his blood,

Hebrews 5:9 NIV 9. and, once made perfect, he became the source of eternal salvation for all who obey him.

Philippians 1:6 NIV 6. Being confident of this, that he who began a good work in you will carry it on to completion until the day of Christ Jesus.

Ephesians 5:1 NIV 1. Follow God's example, therefore, as dearly loved children.

Ephesians 2:9 NIV 9. Not by works, so that no one can boast. Romans 10:9–11 NIV 9. If you declare with your mouth, "Jesus is Lord," and believe in your heart that God raised him from the dead, you will be saved. 10. For it is with your heart that you believe and are justified, and it is with your mouth that you profess your faith and are saved. 11. As Scripture says, "Anyone who believes in him will never be put to shame.

Romans 10:5 NIV 5. Moses writes this about the righteousness that is by the law: "The person who does these things will live by them.

Matthew 16:1–7 NIV 1. The Pharisees and Sadducees came to Jesus and tested him by asking him to show them a sign from heaven.

2. He replied, "When evening comes, you say, 'It will be fair weather, for the sky is red,' 3. And in the morning, 'Today it will be stormy, for the sky is red and overcast.' You know how to interpret the appearance of the sky, but you cannot interpret the signs of the times. 4. A wicked and adulterous generation looks for a sign, but none will be given it except the sign of Jonah." Jesus then left them and went away. 5. When they went across the lake, the disciples forgot to take bread. 6. "Be careful," Jesus said to them. "Be on your guard against the yeast of the Pharisees and Sadducees."

7. They discussed this among themselves and said, "It is because we didn't bring any bread."

1 Corinthians 6:9–10 NIV 9. Or do you not know that wrongdoers will not inherit the kingdom of God? Do not be deceived: Neither the sexually immoral nor idolaters nor adulterers nor men who have sex with men 10. Nor thieves nor the greedy nor drunkards nor slanderers nor swindlers will inherit the kingdom of God.

Romans 10:6–8 NIV 6. But the righteousness that is by faith says: "Do not say in your heart, 'Who will ascend into heaven?'"[a] (that is, to bring Christ down) 7. "Or 'Who will descend into the deep?'"[b] (that is, to bring Christ up from the dead). 8. But what does it say? "The word is near you; it is in your mouth and in your heart,"[c] that is, the message concerning faith that we proclaim:

For our exhortation does not come from error or impurity or by way of deceit; but just as we have been approved by God to be entrusted with the gospel, so we speak, not as pleasing men, but God who examines our hearts.

1 Thessalonians 2:3–4

QUESTIONS YOU NEED TO ASK YOURSELF

1. Do you believe in God and what Jesus has done for you?
2. Do you think that the things we have done will keep us out of heaven or out of his grace? Jesus did not go to the Cross for our sins to be mocked. His promise is real.
3. Have you ever received a Gift or Gifts from God? If so are you using them for Gods Plan within the body of Christ?
4. Have you ever shared your testimony? Will you if it means bringing someone comfort and hopefully to God?
5. How do you think the Holy Spirit works through you? Have you ever felt the Holy Spirit?
6. Do you ever fall into your old nature since you have asked forgiveness?
7. Have you ever felt lost physically? Spiritually? What do you think feels different between the two?
8. How do you look at life compared to heaven and hell?
9. What's the next step in your journey?
10. Prayer is a conversation between you an our Lord, He is always listening, He loves you always not just part of the time and you can tell him everything, Do you pray? I pray you will come to the Lord! Read John 3:16 and Please believe.